MW00425508

1 — SELF CONTROL · GOODNESS · TRUTH · PERFECTION · CLARITY · JUSTICE

2 — HELPFULNESS · ALTRUISM · LOVING · BOLD · SERVANTS HEART · DISCERNING NEEDS

3 — EFFICIENCY · ACTION · ENCOURAGER · ESTABLISHER · INSPIRING · EXCELLENCE

4 — CREATIVITY · EMPATHY · LOVE OF BEAUTY · SPACE SAVER · EMOTIONALLY HONEST

5 — WISDOM · VISION · STEADFASTNESS · CLARITY · FAITHFULNESS · HUMILITY

6 — COURAGE · GUARDIANSHIP · KINDNESS · LOYALTY · STRENGTH · FAITHFULNESS

7 — SPONTANEITY · JOY · THANKFULNESS · HOPE · LONG SUFFERING · VISION

8 — STRENGTH · ZEAL · VIGILANT · JUSTICE · PROTECTOR · TENDERNESS

9 — PEACE · KINDNESS · EMPATHY · PATIENCE · GENTLENESS · UNDERSTANDING

WHAT PEOPLE ARE SAYING ABOUT ELISABETH BENNETT AND *THE ENTHUSIAST: GROWING AS AN ENNEAGRAM 7*

This Enneagram Seven devotional hits the spot for Sevens who are looking to bring healing change to their biggest life struggles and relationships. I love how Elisabeth helps a busy Seven find rest in Christ in a beautiful way, releasing them for the truest joy of the soul.

—*Christa Hardin*
Author and founder, Enneagram + Marriage

Elisabeth has created an invaluable resource for those of us who might struggle a bit more with devoting sixty days to…anything. As an Enneagram Seven, I was inspired by each shift in focus as I often look for the temporary and Elisabeth brings us back to the abiding.

—*Jamie B. Golden*
The Popcast Podcast

Elisabeth has written a delightful devotional full of important information for those who want to grow in their own self-awareness and relationship with Christ. I highly recommend reading this book so you can experience transformation on a much deeper level that will bring about the change you desire in life.

—*Beth McCord*
YourEnneagramCoach.com
Author of 10 Enneagram books

Elisabeth has a beautiful way of guiding the reader into a deeper understanding and self-awareness that leads to spiritual growth through the Enneagram. Through biblically sound and practical devotions, she helps you move from, "Okay, I know what type I am but what's next?" to personal, relational, and spiritual growth, so that you can live in the fullness of who you were created to be in your unique type.

—*Justin Boggs*
The Other Half Podcast
Enneagram coach, speaker, entrepreneur

Through her beautifully articulate words, Elisabeth accurately portrays the shadow side of each Enneagram type while also highlighting the rich grace and freedom found in the spiritual journey of integration. Pairing Scripture with reflection questions and prayers, the devotions help guide the reader on the pathway of personal and spiritual growth in a powerful way that is unique to their type.

—*Meredith Boggs*
The Other Half Podcast

If you know your Enneagram type and you're ready to make meaningful steps toward growth, this book is for you. Elisabeth combines her Enneagram expertise with her deep faith to guide readers toward self-understanding, growth, and transformation through contemplative yet practical writing. This devotional is a great tool that you'll return to again and again.

—*Steph Barron Hall*
Nine Types Co.

60-DAY
ENNEAGRAM DEVOTIONAL

the
ENTHUSIAST

GROWING AS AN ENNEAGRAM

ELISABETH BENNETT

WHITAKER
HOUSE

Introduction images created by Katherine Waddell.
Photo of Elisabeth Bennett by Jena Stagner of One Beautiful Life Photography.

THE ENTHUSIAST
Growing as an Enneagram 7

www.elisabethbennettenneagram.com
Instagram: @enneagram.life
Facebook.com/enneagramlife

ISBN: 978-1-64123-576-1
eBook ISBN: 978-1-64123-577-8
Printed in the United States of America
© 2021 by Elisabeth Bennett

Whitaker House
1030 Hunt Valley Circle
New Kensington, PA 15068
www.whitakerhouse.com

Library of Congress Cataloging-in-Publication Data (Pending)

1 2 3 4 5 6 7 8 9 10 11 **ᴡ** 28 27 26 25 24 23 22 21

DEDICATION

To all the Sevens holding this devotional,
Christ is taking care of you and will never leave you.

Contents

FOREWORD

Seven years ago, I was sitting in our loft reading a book on the Enneagram. I had started to hear more and more about the Enneagram, and I was determined to discover my number. I was told the best way to learn my number was to actually read about all the numbers and whichever number made me squirm might be my number.

Because I am a good student—and thought, *Am I a type Three?*—I read the book from cover to cover to discover my magical number. For several chapters, I resonated deeply with the Perfectionist, type One. I felt really great about my number being a type One. I do love lists, I tend to see things in black and white, and I want things done a certain way. I thought, *I am a type One for sure.*

I was feeling really great about myself. Some people take years to discover their type, but I figured it out in a few, short chapters. Send me my Enneagram gold ribbon please!

And then I got to the chapter on the Enthusiast, type Seven. The first sentence said something along the lines of, "People who are type Seven use joy to escape pain." I burst into tears…and this was very odd because I do not burst into tears. Ever. I didn't understand why my body was responding in such a bizarre way.

I put the book down. I didn't revisit the Enneagram for almost two years. When people asked me what I thought my number was, I let them know I wasn't exactly sure. "But probably type One. Would you like to see my lists?" Some people pointed out my joy, and I let them know my joy was probably very connected to my lists!

For my whole life, I have been defined by my joy. People constantly ask me if it's possible to be as happy as I am. I've always thought this was weird because I haven't ever felt like I was over the top with my happiness. I thought my happiness vibes were completely normal.

And then one day when I was in college, my wallet was stolen. A few hours later, my boyfriend broke up with me. Soon afterward, I discovered that someone had scratched my car and did not have the courtesy to leave a note. It felt like a very bad day. A what-else-can-go-wrong type of day.

I drove to my local smoothie shop, walked in feeling as sad as ever, and ordered my smoothie. After the cashier took my order, she said, "Thank you for smiling and being so cheerful. No one has smiled at me all day."

I was completely shocked. Was I smiling? Was I cheerful? My mood was the exact opposite. I was paying for my smoothie with the few dollars I had left in my pocket, given that my credit card was in my wallet. My stolen wallet. And I could not call my boyfriend for help because today was a good day, in his opinion, to not be my boyfriend. I had not even realized I was smiling as I ordered my smoothie. But there it was.

Maybe my happiness was a little outside the normal zone?

This moment has stayed with me for years because it was indication that perhaps my joy is a bit different from other people's joy. Maybe people are shocked by my joy because it's more abnormal than I realize. And from there on out, joy became my identity. My name is Bri and I am joyful. Apparently, even on really bad days, I am joyful. Other people might be known for their looks, or smarts, or wealth, but I am known by my joy! This is who I am.

Several years later, when I was propped up in my loft with a highlighter and a notebook and an author had the audacity to suggest that maybe my joy—this foundation upon which I set my whole personality—was to escape from pain, my body had a physical response I could not foresee or contain. And my response was complete denial. I am joyful because "I've got the joy, joy, joy, joy down in my heart." Just like the old gospel song says! The joy of the Lord is down in my heart. That's why I'm joyful. That's why I haven't felt pain in years.

You can probably see where this is going.

Two years later, I was back on the Enneagram train, as was the whole world. The first gift the Enneagram gave me was to pay attention to my motivations. Why do I make the decisions I make? I decided to try a little experiment to confirm that I am in fact a type One and not a type Seven. I decided to look at every decision I would make over the next thirty days and find the motivation behind each one. Was I making decisions based on right or wrong...or was I making decisions to escape from pain?

These are a few decisions I made from big to small:

+ Leaving my house at 2:00 p.m. to get a coffee because I need a pick-me-up! Wait, is that the real motivation? Why am I getting coffee? I did just have a hard call with my boss. I'm feeling a little sad and I don't really want to dive into that work project. *Motivation:* I am getting coffee because I am sad and I want something to make me happy…and I am avoiding work.

+ Jeremy is deployed and I have carefully and successfully scheduled trips and evenings out for his whole deployment. *Motivation:* if I am alone, I will think about how much I miss Jeremy and I will probably cry. If I start to cry, I am not sure if I will stop. I do not want to cry. Being around people will help me not miss Jeremy!

+ A friend calls me and tells me some really hard news. I start to feel very sad. But then, I remember the silver lining! This is hard *but* it is only temporary. This too shall pass. Look at the bright side. At least you are still, like, breathing. Yes! At least you are alive. Brilliant. Ok, good talk. Bye. *Motivation:* I would like to think I wanted to cheer my friend up, but I realize I did not want to feel her pain. I could not just sit with her. I brought her a silver lining so I could also retreat to the silver lining.

For thirty days, I really did analyze the motivations for all of my decisions. I realized I make a lot of decisions to avoid pain, from the smallest pain to the biggest. This was not a great discovery, as now I had to figure out what this meant about my joy. Has my joy always been fake? Has it always been an escape route? *Who am I if I am not my joy?*

Through the Enneagram, the Holy Spirit helped me see that my joy was not all bad or all good. Using joy to avoid pain did not mean my joy was corrupt or deceiving. It just meant I leaned heavily on that gift from God to survive and make sense of the world. Joy became my protection, my weapon, and my home base. I used it in all seasons of life for all matter of distraction, avoidance, coping, and enjoyment. And once I understood this, the Holy Spirit was able to refine me in ways I never thought possible. I recognized unhealthy patterns in my life. For example, making all life decisions to avoid pain keeps me from a life of vulnerability and depth in relationships. And while it was eye-opening, I wasn't pleased to realize that I truly hate when my freedom is restricted. My thinking is along the lines of, *Why have one drink when you can have two?! Why invite one family over to your cookout when you can invite the whole neighborhood?! Why order one appetizer for dinner when you can order all the appetizers?!*

And the revelations just keep coming. They're not all *bad* or corrective. Some of them make me feel so honored. I know I am incredibly resilient. I know I am uniquely positioned to deal with social justice issues. I know I can help people celebrate their own lives and accomplishments.

I've done a lot of inner work, yet there is still so much further to go, which is why I am beyond grateful that Elisabeth wrote this sixty-day Enneagram devotional for type Sevens. No matter how many books on devotions you have read or how many podcasts you have listened to on the Enneagram, this devotional will plunge you deep into your soul places. You will emerge a little tender and a little more awake, and you will have uncovered treasure within yourself.

Your joy is from God and it is holy. Your joy is not corrupted just because you have found a few clever ways to wield it to stay afloat in this world. Your joy reflects God's joy, and the world needs you very much.

In this devotional, you will see how your joy can become fuller, brighter, and sharper, and how it can guide you to a place of deeper, richer relationships.

—*Bri McKoy*
Author, *Come & Eat: A Celebration of Love and Grace*
Around the Everyday Table

ACKNOWLEDGMENTS

My journey from young hopeful writer, all the way back to the tender age of four, to holding books with my name on them hasn't been easy or pretty. In fact, it's held a lot of hurt, disappointment, and rejection. However, as you hold a book with my name on the cover in your hands, I'd love you to know who and what has sustained me through it all. You are holding a piece of God's redemption in my story, tangible proof of His kindness, and testament of His faithfulness. I didn't break any doors down or *do* anything myself that ensured my trajectory of publishing. God in His kindness handed me this opportunity, and to Him alone belongs all the glory and praise.

My agent Amanda deserves the highest of thanks and admiration. Thank you for answering my many questions, guiding, and giving me the confidence to do this. I couldn't have done it without you. To all the people at Whitaker House, my editor Peg and publisher Christine, thank you for making these devotionals what they are today. It's been a pleasure working with you all.

To my writing community hope*writers, thank you for giving me the courage to call myself a writer long before I felt like one. Thank you to Pastor Bubba Jennings at Resurrection Church for reading over my proposal and giving me advice on how to serve Jesus well in this process.

The people who have been the biggest support and help to me during this process, and if I'm honest, my life, are:

Molly Wilcox, thank you so much for being a part of this project! I'm so grateful to have met you through the crazy world of social media and grateful that you volunteered to run @7ish_andiknowit. You're a true sweetheart and bright light to those of us who have the pleasure to know you. Thank you for putting your heart into this devotional and for loving your fellow Sevens so well.

To all the other Sevens in my life who have left a big impact on my heart, as well as my ability to write this devotional: John W. Bennett, Julie Upton, Jamie B. Golden, Bri McCoy, all of my Enneagram Seven clients, and a couple other suspected Sevens whom I won't publicly *type* here. Thank you!

Sarah Upton, thank you for faithfully helping with Wellington during this entire journey. I am so comfortable when he is with you, and I adore how much you love him.

Mikayla Larson, thank you for your friendship, support, and for being here when I've needed you the most. You are such a gift in my life.

John and Jan Bennett, thank you for faithfully praying for me and supporting me through this entire process. Your encouragement has moved mountains and sustained me on the hardest days.

Thank you, Mom and Dad (Joe and Diane Upton), for literally teaching me to read and write and encouraging me to say yes to big things. I would never have had the foundation to say yes without you and how you raised me. I'm so proud and grateful to have the two of you in my corner cheering me on.

Peter, you've been beyond supporting, patient, and caring toward me. You have taught me so much about what it means to be faithful, and you never let me quit. You believe in me enough for both of us, and I can't believe the gift that you are in my life. You're my best friend and I love you.

INTRODUCTION
What Is the Enneagram?

The Enneagram is an ancient personality typology for which no one really knows the origins.

It uses nine points within a circle—the word itself means "a drawing of nine"—to represent nine distinct personality types. The points are numbered simply to differentiate between them, with each point having no greater or less value than the others. The theory is that a person assumes one of these personalities in childhood as a reaction to discovering that the world is a scary, unkind place that is unlikely to accept their true self.

The nine types are identified by their numbers or by these names:

1. The Perfectionist
2. The Helper
3. The Achiever
4. The Individualist
5. The Thinker
6. The Guardian
7. The Enthusiast
8. The Challenger
9. The Peacemaker

HOW DO I FIND MY TYPE?

Your Enneagram type is determined by your main motivation. Finding your Enneagram type is a journey, as we are typically unaware of our motivations and instead focus on our behaviors. Many online tests focus on behaviors, and while some motivations *may* produce certain behaviors, this may not always be the case, and you are unlikely to get accurate results.

To find your Enneagram type, you need to start by learning about *all* nine Enneagram types and explore their motivations in contrast to your own behaviors and deeper motivations.

You can ask for feedback from those around you, but most often, the more you learn, the clearer your core number shines through.

It's often the number whose description makes you feel the most *exposed* that is your true core type. Your core Enneagram number won't change, since it's solidified in childhood.

Each number's distinct motivation:

1. Integrity – Goodness
2. Love – Relationships
3. Worth – Self-Importance
4. Authenticity – Unique Identity
5. Competency – Objective Truth
6. Security – Guidance
7. Satisfaction – Freedom
8. Independence – Control
9. Peace – Equilibrium

IS THIS JOURNEY WORTH IT?

Yes! The self-awareness you gain along the way is gold, and learning about the other types in the process brings you so much empathy and understanding for all of the other personalities in your life.

WHAT MAKES THE ENNEAGRAM UNIQUE AND DIFFERENT FROM MYERS-BRIGGS, STRENGTHSFINDER, OR DISC ASSESSMENTS?

The Enneagram, unlike other typology systems, is fluid. Yes, the Enneagram tells you what your base personality characteristics are, but it also reveals how you change when you're growing, stressed, secure, unhealthy, healthy, etc.

You are not the same person at twenty as you are at sixty. You're not the same person at your stressful workplace as you are when binge-watching your favorite TV show and eating ice cream at home. The Enneagram accounts for these inconsistencies and changes in your behavior and informs you of when or how those changes occur.

If you look at the following graph, you'll see that each of the numbers connects to two other numbers by arrows. The arrow pointed toward your number is your growth arrow; the arrow pointed away is your stress number. When your life leaves you with more room to breathe, you exhibit positive characteristics of your growth number, and when you're stretched thin in seasons of stress, you exhibit the negative characteristics of your stress number.

This is one explanation for big shifts in personality over a lifetime.

Another point of difference between the Enneagram and other typology systems is *wings*. Your wings are the two numbers on either side of your core number, which add flavor to your per-

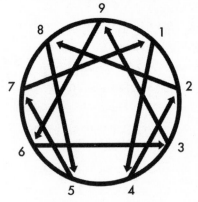

sonality type. Although your core number won't change—and your main motivation, sin proclivities, and personality will come from that core number—your wings can be very influential on your overall personality and how it presents itself. There are many different theories about wings, but the viewpoint we hold to is:

+ Your wing can only be one of the two numbers on either side of your number. Therefore, you can be a 7 with a 6 wing (7w6) but not a 7 with a 5 wing (7w5).

+ You have access to the numbers on either side of your number, but most people will only have one dominant wing. (*Dominant* meaning you exhibit more of the behaviors of one wing than the other wing.) It is possible to have equal wings or no wing at all, but this is rare.

+ Your dominant wing number can change from one to the other throughout your life, but it's speculated this might only happen once.

As you read through this book, we will go over what an Enneagram Seven looks like with both of its wings. If you're struggling to figure out what your core number is, this book series could really help give you some more in-depth options!

HOW DO YOU BECOME YOUR TYPE?

Personality is a kind of shield we pick up and hide behind. It is functional, even protective at times, but altogether unnecessary because God made us in His image from the start. However, we cling to this personality like it's our key to survival, and nothing has proven us wrong so far. It's the only tool we've ever had, and the shield has scratches and dents to prove its worth.

Not all parts of our personality are wrong or bad, but by living in a fallen, sinful world, we all tend to distort even good things in bad ways. Amen?

What personality did you pick up in childhood? If you're reading this devotional, then you may have chosen type Seven. Your need to pursue the things that you think will bring you true satisfaction became the one thing that your life would rotate around from early in childhood up until right now, at this very moment.

The Enneagram talks about childhood wounds and how we pick up a particular shield as a reaction to these wounds. However, not all siblings have the same Enneagram type even though they heard the same wounding message or had the same harmful experiences growing up. This is because we are born with our own unique outlook on the world, and we filter everything through that outlook. You and your siblings may have heard the same things, but while you heard, "No one is going to take care of you," your sibling heard, "You're only loved when you're successful." Thus, you both would become different Enneagram types.

Trauma and abuse of any kind can definitely impact your choice of shield as well. If you think of all these nine shields as being a different color, perhaps you were born predisposed to be more likely to pick blue than red. However, in a moment of early trauma, you might have heard someone shouting, "Pick black! Black is the only option!" Thus, you chose black instead of blue, which would've been your own unique reaction to your life circumstances. It's hard to say how these things happen exactly, especially when trauma is involved. Are you who you are *despite* trauma…or because of it? Only God knows, but there is healing and growth to be found either way.

We've all heard the phrase, "You can't teach an old dog new tricks." I'd like to propose that when referencing personality, it might be said, "The longer you use your personality, the harder it is to see its ineffectiveness." It's not impossible for an older person to drastically change for the better, but it will be harder for them to put down what has worked for them for so long. That's why, as we age, it can become harder to even see where our personality ends and our true self begins. Even if the unhealthy parts of our personality have been ineffective, they still seem to be the only things that have worked for us.

WHY WOULD WE NEED THE ENNEAGRAM WHEN WE HAVE THE HOLY SPIRIT AND THE BIBLE TO GUIDE US?

The Enneagram is a helpful tool, but only when it is used as such. The Enneagram cannot save you—only Jesus can do that.

However, God made us all unique, and we all reflect Him in individual ways. Learning about these unique reflections can encourage us, as well as point us toward our purposes. The Enneagram also reveals the sin problems and blind spots you may unknowingly struggle with. Revealing these blind spots leads us to repentance and change before God.

HOW DO I CHANGE MY MORE NEGATIVE BEHAVIORS?

Alcoholics Anonymous was really on to something when they called their first step "admitting you have a problem." How do you solve a problem if you don't know you have one or are in denial about it? You can't. If you have a shield you're using to protect yourself from the world, but are blissfully unaware of its existence, you won't understand how its very existence impacts you and your relationships. You definitely won't be putting that battered but battle-tested shield of a personality down anytime soon.

Similar to the wisdom of admitting one has a problem before recovery can begin, the Enneagram proposes self-knowledge as the starting point before there can be change.

As a Seven, it may feel a little obvious which shield you picked up. Whether someone has told you you're a Seven, or it became obvious to you on your own, Sevens are often easy to spot.

Whether you're 100 percent sure you are a Seven, or just curious about the possibility, this is what it looks like to be a Seven.

WHAT IT MEANS TO BE
AN ENTHUSIAST

Growing up, Molly was just as passionate about multiple things as she is today. Young Molly could be found spending her free time in as many extracurricular activities as she could fit in her day, from playing sports to playing musical instruments to performing in dance and more.

Molly thrived on learning something new and all the excitement that came with it. She also enjoyed making new friends and the community experience of being on a team. However, with these passions also came a secret sense of shame. You see, Molly would quit things just as easily as she joined them, especially after she had mastered the new skill or experienced all the nuances of whatever she was participating in. There were too many other things to try and too little time to fit everything in, so she often found herself dropping something she'd done for a while, something she had mastered, for something new and fun.

Even if people didn't say it out loud, Molly knew people didn't understand how she could be passionate about some venture, only to quit and move on to something else. She knew people viewed her as a quitter. Molly wished she was like other people who had their *one passion* and stuck with it. She knew being more like the other kids would remove the scarlet letter Q (quitter) from her back and the weight of shame from her shoulders.

Molly is an Enneagram Seven, and as she learned this about herself in college, she could start to look back at her life with a smile and understanding. "Oh, little Seven," she told herself, "you were just being yourself, and your enthusiasm is a gift."

There's a good reason why most Enneagram teachers refer to type Seven as the Enthusiast. Sevens look at life with optimism, energy, and a sense of adventure. They want to experience everything they can, and fun is always on the menu. A healthy Seven is a bright light and a breath of fresh air to our world, while the rest of us are all looking down at our phones, only dreaming of the experiences that Sevens make into reality.

Contentment is the virtue of a healthy Seven. It brings the idea of *finding the joy right here and right now* to the Seven's already happy disposition. A Seven is always going to be up for an adventure, but a healthy Seven no longer relies on the excitement of what's next to be happy. Instead they can rest in the joy that comes from Christ and be happy whether their next adventure is around the corner or not.

A healthy Seven will have forgiven those whom they feel abandoned them in childhood. Such Sevens have processed that deep wound in their own way, finding forgiveness a hard but necessary part of life. This forgiveness has only added to the carefree nature that Sevens have, a nature from which they no longer have to run away.

Sevens are so much fun that the rest of us enjoy spending time with them—even unhealthy or slightly unhealthy Sevens whom we instinctively know are not dependable in the long run.

If you ever watch the A&E television show *Intervention*, you'll see *many* interviews where a family member describes their loved one as a life-of-the-party, happy, and carefree individual. It's baffling that such a person would become a drug addict, thief, or prostitute. However, the Enneagram tells us that Sevens— like Fours and Sixes—can have addictive personalities. Their impulse control issues, combined with pain avoidance, can create the perfect addiction storm when they're unhealthy.

However, few Sevens will say they can relate to being that unhealthy. More commonly, an average or slightly unhealthy Seven will have impulse control issues, they'll forget or disregard commitments, they'll sabotage relationships, and they'll overindulge in almost anything that's exciting.

ALL ABOUT BEING A SEVEN

MOTIVATION

To Be Satisfied

This motivation leads Sevens to pursue the things they think will bring them happiness and true satisfaction in life.

BIGGEST FEAR

Being Deprived or in Pain

Deprivation is the opposite of being satisfied, while pain is an emotion so deep that Sevens wonder if they'll drown in its depths. Sevens avoid negative emotions as much as possible.

HEAD TRIAD

Each Enneagram type is dominant in either feeling, thinking, or doing. These *triads* are referred to as heart-centered, head-centered, and gut-centered.

Sevens, along with Fives and Sixes, are considered to be part of the head triad. This means that they receive all information as something that needs to be thought over and analyzed before they can trust their feelings or gut with processing it. Analysis paralysis, dread, mental exhaustion, and anxiety are some things that this triad can struggle with as they experience the world headfirst. This is the most pronounced in Sevens, as they take information in as something to analyze, and then move on to feeling. In comparison, Sixes analyze their analysis and Fives move on quickly to action.

CHILDHOOD WOUND

The wounding message Sevens heard (or thought they heard) in childhood is, "It's not okay to depend on anyone for anything," or "No one is going to take care of you." Sevens, not having the nurturing support they craved, learned to go into their minds—as a sort of safe play space—to find distractions from their fear and pain.

A Seven might have heard this wounding childhood message if a parent, guardian, or authority figure said, "You're on your own," "I can't help you right now," "You need to learn to do things for yourself," or was otherwise unavailable. Even though this adult may have been neglectful, it's likely that they withdrew affection simply in an effort to help the Seven mature and gain independence, or the adult had another child they needed to help.

THE LOST CHILDHOOD MESSAGE SEVENS LONG TO HEAR

"You Will Be Taken Care Of"

The message "You will be taken care of" takes the weight of responsibility off of the Seven and gives it to Jesus, where it belongs. He will take care of His children, and Sevens don't need to fear pain, boredom, or being abandoned by Him.

DEFENSE MECHANISM

Rationalization

Rationalization is considered to be the preferred defense mechanism of type Sevens. It's used to deal with pain, disappointment, and worries by focusing or *spinning* negative situations into positive ones. This defense mechanism is unproductive when the negative situation isn't processed or dealt with, but rather just dismissed.

WINGS

A wing is one of the numbers on either side of your Enneagram number that adds some *flavor* to your type. You'll still be your core number in essence, but your wing can impact a lot of your behaviors.

Seven with a Six Wing (7w6)

A Seven with a Six wing tends to be playful, friendly, and more cautious than the average Seven. A Six wing can make a Seven be a little less scattered than they might be otherwise. Having this wing often helps Sevens stick with relationships through tough times because the Six's strength is loyalty.

Sevens with a Six wing have lots of optimism and charm, but anxiety will never be too far under the surface. There's an inner tension between the spontaneity of being an Enthusiast and the voice of caution that their Six wing brings. This tension often leads to overthinking and overplanning, things that only those closest to the Seven can see.

Seven with an Eight Wing (7w8)

Sevens with an Eight wing are *high energy*, bold, and fun individuals. They usually have the positivity, lust for adventure, and pain avoidance typical for Sevens, only with much more confidence and social forwardness. An Eight wing can give a Seven a more assertive view on fun, and these Sevens usually finding themselves in the role of a leader in sports or games. Sevens with an Eight wing can often find themselves so bored with projects that they once considered exciting that they quit without finishing them.

Their inner tension is between their core number wanting the freedom to be a spontaneous, fun-loving individual, and their Eight wing's need to be seen as strong and respectful. Obviously, these two needs can coexist, but respect brings with it a lot of responsibility that can make a freedom-loving individual antsy.

ARROWS

The arrows are the two numbers your number is connected to in the Enneagram diagram. These two arrows represent the number from which you get the best traits as you grow, or the number from which you get the worst traits when you're in seasons of stress.

Stress: Going to One

In stress, happy-go-lucky Sevens start to act like an unhealthy One. They'll become critical perfectionists, frustrated with themselves or whoever is around.

Growth: Going to Five

In growth, Sevens will start picking up the behaviors of a healthy Five. They'll be focused, better with personal boundaries, and more content, both with what they have and with the mundaneness of everyday life.

TYPE SEVEN SUBTYPES

When we talk about subtypes and the Enneagram, we are referring to three relational instincts we all have. These instincts, like those of fight or flight, are reactions over which we have little control. The three relational subtypes are Self-Preservation (Sp), Social (So), and One-to-One (Sx). We all have the capacity to use all three of these instincts, but one of them is usually dominant. That dominant subtype can strongly impact how your distinct Enneagram type looks to the rest of us.

The "Here I Go Again" Seven (Sp)

"Mamma Mia!" Cue the ABBA song. The self-preservation Seven is very aware of their own wants and needs; they are also pretty smooth at getting what they want, even if that means talking themselves into splurging, running away, or anything else that would ease the discomfort in their lives.

These Sevens love having a group of friends to do things with, but the group is almost never ideal. Thus, self-preservation Sevens can often sabotage their friendships to protect themselves before these relationships fall apart. This subtype of Seven is the least likely to mistype—that is to say, it's fairly obvious that they are Sevens.

The Caregiver Seven (So)

The social subtype is considered Seven's counter-type because they take on an almost anti-gluttony stance and instead focus their energy on making those around them comfortable and happy. This Seven is most likely to mistype as a Two because of their warmth and the way they articulate wanting to help. Because the Seven's deadly sin of gluttony is still knocking at the door, social Sevens seem to have a very harsh view on anything excessive, even coming across as critical to others when they are really trying to rein in themselves.

The Dreamer Seven (Sx)

The one-to-one Seven is often confused with a type Four because of their creativity, daydreaming, and deep nature. This Seven likes to keep moving and their creative nature can come up with a seemingly unending number of exciting ideas. More assertive than the other two subtypes, this Seven isn't afraid to go after what they want. Relationships are important to this Seven, and they like to have a partner who is just as excited about the world and its possibilities as they are.

SO I'M A SEVEN. WHAT NOW?

Why should I, as a type Seven, embark on sixty days of devotions?

If you have just realized you are a type Seven on the Enneagram, or have come to terms with that reality, you've probably thought at one point or another, *Okay, but what now? I get that I'm an enthusiast, I struggle with contentment, I have a lot of energy, and I love planning the next fun thing I get to do. I might try to avoid negative feelings, but take a chance on things I think will make me happy. The question is, how do I take this self-awareness and turn it into practical transformation?*

Some Enneagram teachers will tell you that you need only to focus on self-actualization and pull yourself up by your proverbial bootstraps to grow out of your worst behaviors. They say things like, "Meditate!" or "Focus on yourself!" or "Sit in your emotion!"

However, I'm here to offer a different foundation for growth. As Christians, we know that we are flawed, sinful, and far from God's intended plan for humanity. The hymn "Come Thou Fount of Every Blessing" includes the lyrics, "Prone to wander, Lord, I feel it." This speaks to the reality of our hearts and their rebellious nature toward our Savior.

This wandering is the problem, sin is the problem, and we are the problem! So, anyone who tells us that we ought to focus on ourselves to find growth will only lead us to more confusion. We may even find ourselves back where we started, as we go around and around this idea of focusing on self.

But we are not without hope. Philippians 1:6 says, *"I am sure of this, that he who began a good work in you will bring it to completion at the day of Jesus Christ."* On the very day you acknowledged Jesus as your Savior, repented from your sin, and dedicated your life to Him, He began a good work in your life. This work is called sanctification, which is the act of becoming holy. Your sanctification will not be finished here on earth, but you are in the process of becoming, day by day, moment by moment, only by the Holy Spirit's work and power within you.

We might not know how to articulate it, but this work of sanctification is the growth and change for which we long. All of us know we are not who we want to be. Reflecting on the human condition in Romans 7:15, Paul said, *"For I do not understand my own actions. For I do not do what I want, but I do the very thing I hate."* Isn't that the truth? I don't want to be angry, but in a world full of flaws, my anger has marked more days than I care to share.

We all know we have this haunting *potential* that always seems just a little out of reach. We all have this nagging feeling that we were created for more…but how do we get there? Only by God's grace and power within us can we rest in His sanctifying work and trust Him for the growth and potential of bringing glory to Him day by day. Only God can sanctify us, but it is our responsibility to be *"slaves of righteousness"* (Romans 6:18) and obey Him.

Over the next sixty days, we want to take you day by day through what God says about *your specific problems as a Seven* and how He wants to lovingly sanctify you into being more like Jesus.

The lens of the Enneagram gives us a great starting point for your specific pain points and strengths. We will use those to encourage you in the areas that God is reflected through you and the areas that you need to lay down your instincts and let Him change you.

Some of these topics might be hard, but we hope that you'll let the tension you feel in your heart open you up to change. This is where our obedience comes in. We all have blind spots and areas we are more comfortable leaving in the dark, but God desires so much more for us. So ask Him to help you release your grip on those areas, bring them into the light, and experience the freedom of repentance.

I'm excited just to write this using words I find diverting
Finding fanciful phrases of bliss, irksome issues, certainly skirting
You see, I tend to choose the brightness, the charming elusive rightness
Fighting for the humor, joy, and lightness even in a dismal crisis

The first to rejoice in triumph and to crack a joke in trials
I'm an ever-loyal comrade seldom seen without a smile
Eager to plan a fun adventure and take a daring flight
Though I may need some help to pinpoint my hurt waiting to ignite

For my highs are insane and my lows are my shame
Seeking shallow comforts to cover up from my pain

Greedy for a thrill I can rack up quite a bill
Never quite believing that I've truly had my fill

Easily filled with wonder in all my bushy-tailed glee
I can seem to some as flimsy a new-sprung baby tree
But those who truly see me, know my roots run far beneath
Insightful and discerning, though my views I often sheath

The expectation of the next excitement can be a magic wand
The freedom to believe that something better is just beyond
Yet I'm thankful for contentment that comes from sitting still
Finding lasting peace within my Savior like the turning of a
windmill

—*John William Bennett*

YOUR GUIDES FOR THIS JOURNEY

You'll be hearing from another writer and Enneagram enthusiast in the days ahead. The days in which no author is listed are written by me. On other days, I have asked an Enneagram expert, who is also a Seven, to help you on your path.

MOLLY WILCOX

Molly Wilcox is the Seven behind the @7ish_andiknowit Instagram account. She has been in love with the Enneagram ever since she first started diving into the system in college. Molly is a writer and spends a lot of her time pouring her heart out into words that uplift and point others to Christ. She currently lives in Tennessee with her husband and adorable miniature Goldendoodle Finley.

10 DAYS OF JOY
How You Uniquely Reflect Christ

DAY 1

What Is Joy?

*But the fruit of the Spirit is love, **joy**, peace, patience, kindness,*
goodness, faithfulness.
(Galatians 5:22)

As an Enthusiast, joy is your trademark. It's natural for you to see the good in almost any situation; you encourage others, and you don't let much get you down.

But what is the difference between true joy and happiness?

"Happiness is completely connected to what's happening to us on the external circumstances of our lives," says Kay Warren, the wife of Pastor Rick Warren of Saddleback Church. "Joy is unrelated to what's happening to us on the outside."

We most clearly see joy when all reasons for happiness are stripped away. This type of joy makes no sense, so we must attribute it to God's goodness and faithfulness.

I had a friend whose cancer journey was marked by both open vulnerability about the difficult journey of dealing with cancer... and his pure joy in Christ. This friend truly counted it all joy, through suffering, trial, and the most unfair cancer diagnosis I've ever seen. Although this friend is in heaven now, the joy of his journey—filled with pain and sickness—is still a vivid reminder to me that God is the Author of joy, not our circumstances.

Joy is a sure feeling deep in your gut that everything is going to be okay and time should not be wasted. Joy is a state of praise toward our Father in heaven, who is in ultimate control. Joy is a fruit of the Spirit, which means God can grow us in joy and He *will* as He is sanctifying us day by day.

Joy, unlike happiness, is not fleeting. Joy is a lifesaver in times of storm and a witness of God's glory to those around us.

SHIFT IN FOCUS

Can you think of an example in your own life where someone was joyful despite their circumstances?

Do you think you are currently pursuing joy or happiness?

• • • • • • • • • • • DAY 2

You Reflect God

And do not be grieved, for the joy of the Lord is your strength.
(Nehemiah 8:10)

Dearest Seven, did you know that you uniquely reflect God? Like seeing your own face staring back at you in a pond, you reflect the image of your heavenly Father. This doesn't mean you have a body that looks like His, but you reflect some of His characteristics to the rest of the world. It's not a perfect reflection; in fact, it's rippled and marred. However, a familiarity, a family resemblance, is still plainly evident between God and His creation. We were made in the image of God.

> *So God created man in his own image, in the image of God he created him; male and female he created them.*
> (Genesis 1:27)

God made us in His image. He didn't have to, but He gave us each unique parts of Himself. Unlike human parents, who don't get to choose their children's genetics, God did decide exactly what He would give us. There is something so special and awe-inspiring about that.

Dear Seven, when you're filled with joy, you reflect part of God to those around. When you hope, you represent our God of hope. When you are long-suffering, you are showing the world the long-suffering of our Father in heaven. There are so many ways God chose to show the world Himself through you!

I find that it's easy to focus on the ways we *don't* reflect God. Our sin is often so loud and shameful, it demands center stage in the thoughts we have about ourselves.

However, have you ever thought about how dwelling on how you reflect God brings glory to Him?

Like a good father beaming at his child, whose love of adventure mirrors his own, God is proud and delighted in the ways we are similar. Thinking about these things, and thanking Him for them, help us to have the right attitude toward ourselves as humans. We are humble, small, fickle, and sinful. And yet we are also adopted, created, and loved beyond measure.

SHIFT IN FOCUS

Spend a couple of moments reflecting on and thanking God for the ways you reflect Him.

Dear heavenly Father, thank You for making me like You. Help me to notice more and more every day the gifts that You have given me, and how I can glorify You with them. I want others to look at me and see a glimmer of You. Thank You for helping me do that. Amen.

My favorite reflection of God that I can see in myself is

_____.

• • • • • • • • • • • **DAY 3**

Sevens Reflect God's Joy

But now I am coming to you, and these things I speak in the world,
that they may have my joy fulfilled in themselves.
(John 17:13)

When we think of God's traits, joy doesn't tend to be very high on the list. Is there even room to have joy when you're holy, righteous, and perfect, looking down at the world with righteous anger?

It can be hard to have a fully conceptualized view of God because we can't imagine being omnipresent, immortal, and... well, God. So we tend to try to make sense of Him in human terms; more often than not, such thinking leads us to an unjust view of who God is.

Yes, God is all of those things we have considered—holy, righteous, perfect, omnipresent, and immortal—*and God is joyful*. Like parents who watch their children do something funny or learn a new skill, I can't help but see God as a proud Father smiling with joy at the trivial triumphs and growth in His beloved children.

God takes joy in the beauty of His creation and the obedience of His children. He may even take joy at some of the amusing aspects of life that He sees, such as a child trying to pronounce a funny word or a cat playing with string. And He freely gives His joy to His children through His Spirit.

We see some of the manifestations of God's joy in the life of Jesus. Jesus wasn't considered to be overly handsome, He wasn't rich, and He didn't naturally have any worldly power or influence. However, He attracted crowds because of who He was and who was working in Him. We do know that Jesus was a joyful person. He was fun, witty, and sarcastic at times. He joked and even played with children, unlike other religious teachers of His day.

Dear Seven, the joy you exude reflects a God who is joyful, fun, and smiling, a God who delights in us. The world doesn't often hear that God is joyful, so your reflection of this aspect of Him is an important honor for you and educates the rest of us.

SHIFT IN FOCUS

As you reflect on the life of Jesus, who displays a life of joy despite His circumstances in all of the gospel accounts, think about your own life and how you experience joy. Consider where you might be missing opportunities to proclaim the glory of the Lord through your joy.

When Jesus said things like, *"Take the log out of your own eye"* (Matthew 7:5), or *"It is easier for a camel to go through the eye of a needle"* (Matthew 19:24), these statements would have been very funny to His audience in that culture.

Can you think of other verses in Scripture in which Jesus is depicted as joyful, where He laughed, joked, or played?

• • • • • • • • • • • **DAY 4**

What the Bible Says About Joy

Rejoice and be glad, for your reward is great in heaven.
(Matthew 5:12)

The Bible is not silent on joy and rejoicing. You'll find a consistent theme throughout both the New and Old Testaments of God's people being called to rejoice and find joy in the Lord. In the Old Testament, we read:

> *Be glad in the LORD, and rejoice, O righteous, and shout for*
> *joy, all you upright in heart!* (Psalm 32:11)

Being commanded to be glad and rejoice might seem to contradict the spirit of joy, but really, we are being commanded to *remember*. Our sinful hearts are quick to forget that our reasons for rejoicing are greater than the momentary pain, afflictions, and cruelty of this world. When we fail to put our pain in its proper place and forget the eternal joy of our salvation, we are indulging in self-pity and foolishness.

This doesn't mean we cannot mourn or have bad days. The Bible even tells us to mourn with those who mourn (see Romans 12:15) and *"bear one another's burdens"* (Galatians 6:2). This world is fallen and sinful; the pain is *real*. But much like grieving for a loved one who is now with Jesus in heaven, all of our pain has a silver lining.

Death is not forever; devastation can be redeemed; the sin of others against you will be taken care of in hell or on the cross of Christ; and Jesus is with you, right here and right now.

Friends, that's more than enough reason to not let our loud feeling overtake the joy that we have in Christ. Joy is not reserved for the good days, the happy times, or when we feel like having a joyful and grateful spirit. If you are in Christ and have been saved for eternity to be with Him, then your joy is for every moment of every day. This is biblical joy.

SHIFT IN FOCUS

Today might feel like an easy day for joy, a day in which you could write gratitude lists as long as your arm. Or maybe joy is hard for you today. Maybe you're praying, *"Restore to me the joy of your salvation"* (Psalm 51:12) and gratitude lists don't reflect your heart's current position.

Wherever you are today, can I encourage you that Jesus is here with you? He is not a God who is far off, but One who is near to you. (See Jeremiah 23:23.)

Let your heart praise Him, even if you don't feel like it. Turn on some worship music and spend some time rejoicing in the Lord.

• • • • • • • • • • • **DAY 5**

Joy and David
By Molly Wilcox

> *You have turned for me my mourning into dancing;*
> *you have loosed my sackcloth and clothed me with gladness,*
> *that my glory may sing your praise and not be silent.*
> *O LORD my God, I will give thanks to you forever!*
> (Psalm 30:11–12)

Dear Seven, people often recognize you for your joy. It is a gift God has stamped on your life, and a gift we Sevens can give to those around us. Despite the trials you face, you can find true joy in Christ.

When I look to God's Word and see the arc of King David's life, I see the many trials he faced. He faced a giant, he was hated and hunted by Saul, he fought many strong armies, and he had to leave friends and his home behind to protect his life. Yet, when we read through the Psalms, we remember David for singing songs of praise.

He credits the Lord for shifting his mourning into dancing, turning his sorrow into joy. In other words, David would look on the bright side. As believers, we can do the same thing in a much deeper way than what the world normally expects. Whether you're facing an illness, a challenging relationship, a difficult financial situation, or a struggle with your job, we have the ability to see God's redemptive purpose and plan throughout our challenges. We have the ability to ask God to *turn our mourning into dancing,* and actually celebrate despite what we are facing.

Has anyone ever asked you, "Why do you always seem so happy?" When I am asked this question, it is often posed in a tone of surprise. Usually, it's because I seem happy or have the ability to laugh or have a good time when the people around me are shocked or overwhelmed by life's circumstances.

So, in quiet reflection, ask yourself, "Why am I so happy?" When I am honest with myself, I know what I am feeling isn't happiness but joy. And it doesn't come from me; it comes from God. No matter the circumstance, I can find joy because I know who God is, and He is redeeming everything. With the help of His Holy Spirit, I can greet even the most difficult day with joy and celebration, just as David did.

SHIFT IN FOCUS

Make a list of any challenges or hardships you are personally facing, or any in the lives of those you love or your community. After you have completed this list, make a note of how you can celebrate God's presence in the midst of each. Ask the Holy Spirit to help you to be a steward of joy in the world today.

• • • • • • • • • • • **DAY 6**

Joy and God's Purpose for You
By Molly Wilcox

And the angel said to them, "Fear not, for behold, I bring you good news of great joy that will be for all the people. For unto you is born this day in the city of David a Savior, who is Christ the Lord."
(Luke 2:10–11)

Dear Seven, you are likely already aware that you are a joyful person. But did you realize God has a purpose for your joy? One of the most astounding times I see joy in Scripture is when the angel comes and promises there will be joy in the world and the joy is brought through Jesus.

When the angel came and made this promise, he promised great joy! Jesus came and walked among us, died for our sins on the cross, and rose again so we could have full access to the Father. The veil was torn, and as a believer in Him, we get to live in eternal celebration! This is truly good news of great joy!

Joy is a promise God made us, a gift from heaven. Joy came into the world, and it is our future. Joy is found in the good news of the Gospels, and joy was a part of God's plan from the very beginning.

As Sevens, God wants us to feel a purpose in our joy. Joy is His gift to you so that you feel near to your Father's heart. Joy tells you in hard circumstances that God is still near and He still has a plan and purpose for your life. We will always have a reason to celebrate because Jesus came to save us, but joy is also part of God's purpose for where you are positioned today.

When you walk into a room and you are truly joyful, you carry the presence of Jesus into that room. You don't even have to say His name; people around you will sense the Spirit of the Lord near to them because God is joyful. When your boss is negative, when your kids won't behave, and when it feels like the world is overwhelming, people will still see this joy in you. And when they see the joy in you, they will see Jesus.

SHIFT IN FOCUS

Spend a few moments in prayer reflecting on the joy of your salvation. Ask the Holy Spirit to highlight ways His joy is impacting your life and community. Invite Him to help you live a life that is purposed in His joy.

• • • • • • • • • • • **DAY 7**

God's Joy in You
By Molly Wilcox

But the fruit of the Spirit is love, joy, peace, patience, kindness,
goodness, faithfulness, gentleness, self-control.
(Galatians 5:22–23)

Dear Seven, have you ever felt pressured to be joyful? I know I have. In social situations, people often view me as *the fun one*. I proudly wear this title and I love that people around me want to invite me to their gatherings, knowing I am fun to be around, usually accompanied by lots of laughter and amusing, detailed stories to share.

But sometimes, it can feel exhausting to be the *fun* friend. Sometimes, I need time and space to just be me, no matter what emotions I may be experiencing. When I rely on my emotions to be happy and fun, I feel like I am a burden when I'm not feeling that way. I am released from the burden to always be happy when I am able to recognize joy for what it is.

Joy is a fruit of the Holy Spirit and comes from God. I cannot be a carrier of joy without being empowered by the Spirit. Therefore, the pressure to be joyful is taken away from me. Joy is given to me by the Lord, and He is the only One who can bring it. I will only be joyful when I take time to encounter the Spirit and allow Him to fill me with joy.

When I am filled with joy from the Spirit of the Lord, I bring so much more to social gatherings than emotions. I bring the presence of the Holy Spirit. Others will recognize His joy in you—and this is of far greater value than a funny story or a joke that lightens a tense mood or breaks an awkward silence.

Wherever you need to be today, know that the pressure isn't on you to be joyful. You can't be filled with joy on your own. The Holy Spirit will fill you with new joy every day; even if you are experiencing other emotions, He will fill you with joy and equip you with joy. Release yourself from the burden to be joyful for others. Instead, know the Holy Spirit can fill them with joy and respond in intercession.

SHIFT IN FOCUS

Spend time asking the Holy Spirit to fill you with God's joy. Think of a circumstance or relationship where you felt a burden to be happy, and release that to Him. Ask Him to enter in and fill that space with His joy. Thank Him for the joy He has given. Thank Him for being the source of joy and for taking away the burden you felt.

• • • • • • • • • • • **DAY 8**

Joy and Helping Others

Do not neglect to do good and to share what you have,
for such sacrifices are pleasing to God.
(Hebrews 13:16)

When you're living in joy, it's easy to think about helping others more often than not because your joy helps you see everything as a gift. Your time, your money, your talents, your possessions—all are gifts from God to be used for His glory and our good. Thinking from this perspective makes the sacrifice of possessions, time, or money to help someone else a no-brainer. You realize that none of these things was really yours to begin with.

Paul tells us, *"Let each of you look not only to his own interests, but also to the interests of others"* (Philippians 2:4).

We don't help others to have our wealth multiplied, to get something in return, or to look good. We help others out of the abundance of our joy because it's pleasing to our heavenly Father and acting out of obedience to Him.

When you help others, you're saying that your time is not worth more than theirs. You're saying that your money belongs to God and not just to you. You're saying that you believe what God says when He tells you that helping others is a good thing.

You may be thinking right now about those in your life who are in need. Perhaps you can't think of anyone and don't even know where to start to find people who could use your help.

However, have you ever felt God nudge you toward donating money to a specific cause or person?

Have you ever felt like you should ask that mom at the grocery store if she needs some help?

Do you often follow through on these nudges from the Lord, or do you ignore them?

The more you say *yes* to the call to help, the more you'll hear the call. You'll become more attuned to God's voice and people will see you as someone who is willing to help. That's no small thing.

To those who are faithful with a little, God will entrust with much, as Jesus taught us.

> His master said to him, "Well done, good and faithful servant. You have been faithful over a little; I will set you over much. Enter into the joy of your master." (Matthew 25:21)

SHIFT IN FOCUS

Think back on an instance in which you ignored a nudge from God. Were you prioritizing your comfort and your time, or were you concerned that you would appear to be naïve or silly? Were you afraid that your offer to help would be rejected?

How have you felt during the times you did say *yes* to the nudge from God to act?

● ● ● ● ● ● ● ● ● ● ● ● **DAY 9**

Joy and Living Gratefully
By Molly Wilcox

> *Let us come into his presence with thanksgiving;*
> *let us make a joyful noise to him with songs of praise!*
> (Psalm 95:2)

When I was walking through a particularly challenging season, a friend encouraged me to begin each day by writing a list of ten things for which I was grateful. In this season, I had been asking God for a lot. I felt I was in a time of need; there were so many things I was praying for and believing He would provide. It was easy to get caught up in all of the things I felt I lacked and spend my time focusing on going to God with my requests.

But as I began to write lists of ten things I was grateful for every day, I quickly noticed how my prior lack of gratitude had stolen my joy. When I took time to be grateful before going to God with my requests, I approached Him differently. With my list of things for which I was thankful, my mind shifted back to being joyful and my spirit felt lighter.

Each day, it became easier to find ten things for my gratitude list and I was constantly reminded of ways God had shown up for me in the past. Instead of seeing how impossible I felt my circumstances were and asking God for more, I was focused on all of the precious gifts He had given me...and I felt more certain of His power to show up for me again.

Without a focus on gratitude, it felt like I was beating on a door, begging and asking God to change things. But when I spent time thanking God first, I felt peaceful confidence in His provision and character. I felt a deep sense of joy within me as I asked my Father to do for me what He has done before and could certainly do again.

There are still days when I may feel like I don't have many reasons to be grateful. On these days, I take the time to remind myself that God has already given me the greatest gift of eternal life, access to Him through His Son, and the presence of His Holy Spirit. Then my focus shifts and I can truly feel a deep sense of gratitude and be filled with His joy.

SHIFT IN FOCUS

Make a list of ten things you can thank God for today. Be detailed and specific. If you don't feel like you have a lot of reasons to thank God, begin by simply thanking Him for who He is. Ask His Holy Spirit to use gratitude to establish joy within you today.

● ● ● ● ● ● ● ● ● ● ● **DAY 10**

Joy and Living on Mission
By Molly Wilcox

And let them offer sacrifices of thanksgiving,
and tell of his deeds in songs of joy!
(Psalm 107:22)

Dear Seven, have you ever thought about how God can use your joy to lead others to Him? One of my favorite things about going to church is hearing people's testimonies. Whether it is in a small group setting or from the stage, I love hearing about what God is doing in other people's lives.

I've noticed that when someone shares a testimony of what God has done for them, it usually begins in a place of uncertainty. They may be up against something they haven't faced before, or they are unsure about what the future holds.

Then, at some point, the story shifts. God shows up and He moves. By the end of the testimony, there is rejoicing and celebration. Everyone is smiling or clapping and recognizing the goodness of God.

God gives us these stories of His goodness to encourage us to tell others about who He is. The result is often joy!

Joy is a gift God has given us to bring glory to Him and lead people to Him. Maybe someone will specifically ask you how you can find joy even when you face trials. You can use that opportunity to share the good news of Jesus Christ.

Perhaps people around you will start to sense there is something unique about your joy. It isn't dependent upon your mood, or what day of the week it is, but there is a genuine presence of joy in your life. Inviting others into that space is another way to invite them to know Jesus. Allow people to witness your joy and be intentional about sharing the source. God has placed you in your community in order for you to share His joy, which can ultimately lead people into a full and fruitful relationship with Him.

SHIFT IN FOCUS

Take time to reflect or journal on a time when someone may have noticed your joy.

Did you take the opportunity to share where your joy comes from? If not, ask the Holy Spirit to give you more opportunities to share your joy to the world around you and ultimately reveal the heart of the Father to a world in need.

If you did tell others that God is the source of your joy, ask the Holy Spirit to continue to draw people into a joy-filled relationship with God. Thank Him for using joy in you and ask Him to give you more opportunities to celebrate the work God is doing for you and those around you.

10 DAYS OF KILLING GLUTTONY

How the Enemy Wants You to Stop Reflecting God

What Is a Deadly Sin?

> *If anyone is caught in any transgression,*
> *you who are spiritual should restore him in a spirit of gentleness.*
> *Keep watch on yourself, lest you too be tempted.*
> (Galatians 6:1)

Although the wording or specific idea for the "seven deadly sins" is not in the Bible, the list of them has been used by Christians for ages. The classification of seven deadly sins that we know today was first penned by a monk named Evagrius Ponticus who lived from AD 345–399.

This list has gone through many changes since its origination, but it has remained a helpful way for us to name the common vices that keep us in chains.

When these seven sins are paired with specific Enneagram numbers (plus two extra sins to make nine), they give us a better idea of the specific vices that may be tripping us up again and again. This is important because these problems are often blind spots in our lives. Their exposure leads us to repentance, better health, and greater unity with Christ, which is the greatest thing learning about our Enneagram number can do for us.

Here are the deadly sins early Enneagram teachers paired with each type:

1. Anger

2. Pride

3. Deceit

4. Envy

5. Greed

6. Fear

7. Gluttony

8. Lust

9. Sloth

Struggling with one of these sins dominantly does not mean that you do not struggle with all of them. If we are honest with ourselves and humble, we can all recognize ourselves in each of the sins listed. However, your dominant deadly sin is a specific tool Satan will use to distract the world from seeing how you reflect God.

For Sevens, the deadly sin you struggle with most is gluttony. Whether or not you recognize gluttony in your own life as you're thinking about it now, I entreat you to give great thought to it in these next ten days.

Exposing blind spots in our life can feel a lot like ripping off a bandage that we might prefer to leave on, but what's underneath is God-honoring and beautiful.

SHIFT IN FOCUS

Spend some time contemplating and praying about what gluttony might look like in your life.

Does it surprise you to see that specific sin printed next to your Enneagram number?

DAY 12 • • • • • • • • • • •

What Is Gluttony?

But watch yourselves lest your hearts be weighed down with dissipation and drunkenness and cares of this life.
(Luke 21:34)

Did you know that gluttony doesn't have to be about food? No, gluttony is much too greedy for your time, money, and affection to just stick to food as a method of stealing your joy and peace.

Gluttony is the sin you're indulging in when you use *anything* excessively, without caring about consequences, or for a high that numbs you to reality.

When you watch TV excessively or without self-control, you're indulging in gluttony. When you go shopping and buy things you can't afford in order to get the *high* from having new things, you are indulging in gluttony. When you sleep in even though you know you'll be rushed or late for work, you're indulging in gluttony. When you know you shouldn't eat the whole box of doughnuts or the entire bag of chips, but you've had a hard day and it'll make you feel better, you're indulging in gluttony.

Gluttony seems harmless...until it's not. It's harmless until you lose your job, can't get out from under credit card debt, or can't lose the weight. Sometimes, the lapse in self-control through gluttony is training you and leading you to bigger and bigger addictions.

Abusing pain medications, playing video games for hours on end, drinking alcohol until you pass out, watching pornography that gets worse and worse, and abusing anything that can make you forget reality for right now—all of these lie at the bottom of the slippery slide of gluttony.

Gluttony is sneaky because it's really good at saying two things:

+ "Just this once."

+ "You deserve this—and you need it."

SHIFT IN FOCUS

How gluttony manifests is as different as each individual Seven, but one thing to keep in mind is that gluttony is often a lonely sport. Temptation strikes hardest when you're alone.

You might get caught up in the fun of shopping with a friend and overspend, but it's different when you're by yourself and shopping to self-medicate.

Spend some time reflecting on how gluttony might be appearing in your life.

Give three examples:

1. _____

2. _____

3. _____

DAY 13 • • • • • • • • • • •

How Satan Uses Gluttony

So, whether you eat or drink, or whatever you do,
do all to the glory of God.
(1 Corinthians 10:31)

Any person can have the potential to sin in any way. However, certain personalities seem to be more tempted by certain sins than others. It's helpful to know what your sin proclivities are so you can take steps to avoid these particular sins.

Satan uses gluttony as a particular tool to keep Sevens dissatisfied. The enemy often tries to entice Sevens to indulge in gluttony through shopping, television, social media, food, sex, alcohol, sleep, pain medications, and any other avenues that tempt you.

Satan whispers, "You'd be happy if only you had this..." or "Just a little more." These are the empty promises of gluttony.

Gluttony is especially derailing to Sevens because it either numbs them or keeps them distracted by fixating on their next high. Sevens reflect God in so many beautiful ways—joy, hope, spontaneity, and long-suffering, just to name a few—and these reflections are on full display when Sevens focus their gifts and talents on living their life for Christ and experiencing His full joy. This is nothing like the momentary false happiness that you get from gluttony.

Satan knows that he may not have your future or eternity, but he is actively trying to steal your impact, your peace, and your joy.

One of the best ways to fight gluttony is to call it what it is: sin. That's why it's harmful to brush off sinful traits as something a little innocent or not so bad. We do this by saying things like, "I'm just having a lazy month," or "Being content is not who I am," or "I like to eat a lot and there's nothing wrong with that," or "I just have impulse control issues."

God says gluttony is a sin, but through the Holy Spirit, we will always find a way to escape the temptation of sin.

> No temptation has overtaken you that is not common to man. God is faithful, and he will not let you be tempted beyond your ability, but with the temptation he will also provide the way of escape, that you may be able to endure it. (1 Corinthians 10:13)

SHIFT IN FOCUS

How do you combat gluttony? Can you see where God is giving you a way to escape it?

Accountability may be a helpful next step if you're struggling with gluttony. As we mentioned yesterday, loneliness usually makes the temptation worse, so ask someone to help you carry this burden.

DAY 14 • • • • • • • • • • •

What Does God Say About Gluttony?

For many, of whom I have often told you and now tell you even with tears, walk as enemies of the cross of Christ. Their end is destruction, their god is their belly, and they glory in their shame, with minds set on earthly things.
(Philippians 3:18–19)

Dear Seven, what are you tempted to make your *god* besides God? Your stomach? Your adrenal gland? Your eyes? Your Amazon shopping cart? You video game score? The number next to your name on Instagram or TikTok?

Paul was writing to the church in Philippi about those who walked as enemies of the cross of Christ. Not as hostile, destructive enemies, but as people whose gazes were fixed on worldly pleasures instead of obedience to Jesus. Paul was in tears as he thought about these brothers and sisters, knowing that they faced destruction and their worldly pleasures would not fill the longing in their souls.

"Their god is their belly," Paul says of these people. Following the temptation of gluttony ultimately led these people to be enemies of Christ. They did not set out to become God's enemies, but they listened to the grumbling of their stomach; its cry for more was louder than the still small whisper of God, so they were led astray.

The wisdom book of Proverbs has a lot to say about gluttony. For example:

> For the drunkard and the glutton will come to poverty, and slumber will clothe them with rags.　　(Proverbs 23:21)

The Bible is clear that gluttony leads to poverty and addiction. Worse still, it leads to separation from God.

When you make something *your god* other than our Creator, God of everything, the Bible calls this idolatry. It's so important to avoid this sin that God made it the first of His Ten Commandments. You cannot dismiss it as being no big deal.

SHIFT IN FOCUS

An easy way to see what you're tempted to make *your god* is to take a look at your priorities. Take a look at your bank account, your calendar, or your phone usage. If someone else looked at these things, what would they say you cared about the most?

DAY 15 • • • • • • • • • • •

Solomon and Gluttony

Now King Solomon loved many foreign women…from the nations concerning which the LORD had said to the people of Israel, "You shall not enter into marriage with them, neither shall they with you, for surely they will turn away your heart after their gods." Solomon clung to these in love. He had 700 wives, who were princesses, and 300 concubines. And his wives turned away his heart.
(1 Kings 11:1–3)

Solomon was the son of King David and heir to the throne of Israel. He was handsome, smart, and probably never lacked anything.

When his father died and Solomon became king, God appeared to him in a dream and said, *"Ask what I shall give you"* (1 Kings 3:5). Solomon did not ask for long life or riches but for *"an understanding mind"* (verse 9). God was so pleased that He gave Solomon *"a wise and discerning mind, so that none like you has been before you and none like you shall arise after you"* (verse 12), as well as wealth and fame.

Solomon had the honor of building a temple for God in Israel. This was an honor David sought, but God told him *no* because David's hands were soaked with blood as a man of war. However, God told David that his son Solomon would build the Lord's house.

Solomon's reign as king was during a time of great wealth and power in Israel. He was esteemed far and wide, had all the wealth he could have ever wanted, and any worldly pleasure within arm's reach.

Before you start to envy Solomon or wish your life were like his, consider these five heartbreaking words in the heading for chapter 11 of the First Book of Kings:

SOLOMON TURNS FROM THE Lord

When I read this, my heart always cries, "What? No! Why?!" Solomon had everything; God had blessed him beyond measure. Solomon spoke to God in a way you and I will probably never experience.

So what happened? Gluttony happened. Solomon had everything, but he still wanted more, and that desire would ultimately lead his heart astray.

You see, Solomon had a problem with gluttony, not just with wealth, chariots, horses, wisdom, fame, and drink—because the Bible talks about all of those things as well—but with women. Solomon is recorded as having 700 wives and 300 concubines, making him perhaps the worst polygamist the world has ever known. And because he clung to all of these women, they turned his heart away from God.

Time and time again, history has shown us that when we have everything, we never feel like we have enough. This isn't just a problem for you, but it's a problem for whoever you idolize or wish you could be as well. Enough is never enough because gluttony only offers the promise of satisfaction without ever delivering.

No possession, experience, or *more* of any kind will ever fill the God-shaped hole in your heart.

SHIFT IN FOCUS

What do you learn from the story of Solomon?

What are you tempted to think you'd be satisfied with if only you had enough of it?

• • • • • • • • • • • DAY 16

Gluttony and Numbing
By Molly Wilcox

Be not among drunkards or among gluttonous eaters of meat,
for the drunkard and the glutton will come to poverty,
and slumber will clothe them with rags.
(Proverbs 23:20–21)

As a Seven, I am so afraid of missing out on something good, I feel the need to try absolutely everything. I am someone who consumes too much, but my problem isn't food. It's often too many episodes on Netflix, too many online orders from favorite boutiques, or too many experiences, from making travel plans and booking flights to overwhelming my calendar with appointments and activities.

As I have learned to recognize these behaviors in myself, I've also learned to recognize some of my triggers. If I had a disappointing day at work, or a conversation took a turn that upset me or left me feeling misunderstood, I may try to avoid that painful emotion. In my best attempt to numb myself, I suddenly fix my focus on a new Netflix series and binge watch the night away to avoid my own aching emotions.

Honestly, I sometimes still believe the lie that numbing myself from pain and consuming more of something in search of satisfaction is an okay way to deal with difficulties in life. The reality is that running from what's bothering you robs you of the fullness of life. By trying to protect yourself, you're actually stealing from yourself.

The Scriptures tell us that the glutton will come to poverty; overconsumption of anything can cost a lot of money. I don't want to spend my life indulging to the point where I am poor in any way, not just financially or physically, but also spiritually. Consuming too much leaves a person tired, worn out, and unable to go about their normal existence effectively. In other words, if we turn to gluttony in order to numb ourselves from pain, we miss out on life. The thing we want to avoid—missing out—is actually caused by our attempt to fix it by consuming too much.

We can hurt ourselves even more when we try to consume and do so much that we leave no space for God's purpose in our lives. For me, this comes in the form of saying yes to everything. I've gone through seasons where *no* isn't in my vocabulary, and I suffer as a result. With a packed schedule, there is no room for God's plans for me; my true calling and purpose are eaten away by unnecessary distractions.

Let's challenge one another to be wiser than Solomon and avoid the sin of gluttony. Starting today, notice your triggers and don't go overboard in an effort to numb your pain.

SHIFT IN FOCUS

Journal about the following:

- What are some ways you consume too much in your life?

- Can you recognize what triggers these gluttonous behaviors?

- In what ways are you numbing yourself from experiencing a full range of emotions?

Respond in prayer by thanking God for sending His Son Jesus Christ to die for your sins. You may want to use this time for confession and repentance. Receive His forgiveness and ask His Holy Spirit to be with you in all of your emotions.

DAY 17 •••••••••••

Gluttony and Discontentment

*Not that I am speaking of being in need, **for I have learned** in whatever situation I am to be content. I know how to be brought low, and I know how to abound. In any and every circumstance, I have learned the secret of facing plenty and hunger, abundance and need. I can do all things through him who strengthens me.*
(Philippians 4:11–13)

These are among my favorite verses in the Bible. I love Paul's zeal and honesty about life! In the entire epistle to the Philippians, he is truthful about how we can make life more difficult for ourselves because we give into our sinful nature, and how easy it can be when we are leaning fully on Christ.

We see in these verses that Paul makes an important clarification about contentment in these four little words: "*for I have learned.*" Paul was not born more prone toward contentment than any of us, and it was also not something supernaturally gifted to him by God. Paul had to *learn* to be content. And how do you learn? By constant practice.

Just like anything else that's hard, contentment is something we wish we could master…without going through the tough work of practicing it. We want to be content, yet we give in when our heart wants something instead of practicing contentment. This is where we get in our own way, and where we need discipline. We need to fight thoughts like these:

+ I want to be content...but the newest version of my phone just came out and mine is *so* slow.

+ I want to be content...but I'm bored with the clothes in my closet and I want something new.

+ I want to be content...but I've had a hard day and there's an online sale I want to check out.

+ I want to be content...but having a new car would make me so happy.

This list could go on and on with my daily temptations toward gluttony instead of contentment.

Contentment looks like saying *no* to yourself. It looks like being present instead of longing for the future. Contentment looks like gratefulness and not comparing what you have to what others have.

Each and every time you chose contentment over gluttony, you're practicing a new skill. One day, like Paul, you will be able to say, *"For I have learned."*

SHIFT IN FOCUS

How would you finish this statement:

I want to be content, but_____.

Is there a practical way that you can practice contentment today?

Pray and ask God to give you a heart that is opposed to gluttony and longs for contentment.

DAY 18 • • • • • • • • • • •

Gluttony and Loneliness

Then the LORD God said, "It is not good that the man should be alone; I will make him a helper fit for him.
(Genesis 2:18)

This verse from Genesis is often used in reference to marriage, but with what we now know about isolation and the human condition, I'd say it has much broader application.

In the beginning, Adam was the *only* human on the entire earth. Talk about isolation! God said this isolation, and Adam's loneliness, was *"not good."* It's the only thing God would pronounce as *not good* before sin would even enter the world. Our very human nature, at its core, knows that we need each other. Even when sin muddies the waters with pain, betrayal, and all the various ways we hurt each other, we still need relationships with people. God made us to *need* each other and made us *for* each other.

When Sevens feel lonely and isolated, gluttony often shows up in full force. Why? Because you are coping with something that feels wrong and you don't want to actually *feel* what's going on.

Sevens I've coached have often said that they have many good friends, but they still suffer from loneliness. Maybe your friends are used to you initiating all contact and making all the plans, which becomes exhausting so you back off...leading to loneliness. Maybe you have a lot of long-distance friends but have yet to make tangible close friends. Maybe your friends are in a busy season of life and not around as much as you need them to be.

Even the friendliest, most extroverted people still will have seasons of loneliness because we don't live in a world where relationships are perfect.

Have grace for your friends, prioritize community, keep making new friends, and keep reaching out. The need for other people is a valid one. Don't let anyone shame you into feeling guilty that you need community because we all do. God does not want us to be alone; in fact, God says it's not good for us to be alone.

SHIFT IN FOCUS

Are you in a season of loneliness?

When during the day are you most likely to feel lonely? Instead of scrolling through social media or indulging in gluttony, it may be smart to have a game plan for that time of the day.

For instance, if Saturday mornings are hard for you, you could FaceTime an old friend for brunch. Maybe nighttime is hard because you live alone. You might consider getting a roommate, or inviting people over for movies or game nights.

DAY 19 • • • • • • • • • • •

Having an Addictive Leaning
By Molly Wilcox

Their end is destruction, their god is their belly, and they glory in their shame, with minds set on earthly things.
(Philippians 3:19)

Before I had the context of the Enneagram, I knew I had an addictive leaning. I often get hooked on something I like or appreciate. If I watch one episode of a new TV show and enjoy it, it quickly turns into an entire season. If I have a free minute, I'll decide to hop on my phone and spend too much time scrolling through various social media platforms. If I start to watch one YouTube video of people teaching fun tricks to their dogs, I can lose an entire afternoon trying to figure out if my dog would be able to skateboard.

Sometimes, we can become addicted to things that aren't necessary bad, but they aren't good or godly when they take a place of idolatry in our lives. In Philippians, we read, *"Their god is their belly,"* and the belly is clearly the one in control here; the desire for food and consumption controls a person and becomes the thing being worshipped. This should be a red flag for us.

Where do you see yourself becoming addicted to things in your life? What are you currently fixated on? Are you letting that addiction control you?

My husband would quickly tell you that I'm addicted to social media. As someone who loves both words and photography,

Instagram is my go-to platform. Of course, I never want to miss out on seeing or posting a great photo and caption. However, addiction to social media can become destructive in my life when it begins to take the place of God. When I start to allow social media to have a place of worship in my life, a place that should be devoted to my heavenly Father, that addictive behavior becomes dangerous.

To combat this, I've found the best way for me to gain freedom from addiction, even a fun one, is fasting. I stay off my phone most Sundays and I intermittently fast from social media for weeks at a time when I feel myself holding it too closely. That effectively takes my eyes away from the earthly desires I have been clinging to and sets my focus back on the Father, where it belongs.

SHIFT IN FOCUS

Do you have addictions that are taking a place of idolatry in your life?

Consider challenging yourself to a season of fasting. Select something you know you overdo, consider a timeframe for fasting from it, and think of one person who can hold you accountable if necessary. Use the time to allow God to speak to you. View this time of fasting not as a time when you have less, but as a time when you have more access to the Father and He has more access to you.

DAY 20 • • • • • • • • • • •

Sobriety and Finding Satisfaction and Comfort in God
By Molly Wilcox

But put on the Lord Jesus Christ,
and make no provision for the flesh, to gratify its desires.
(Romans 13:14)

There are times when I genuinely believe the lie that I'll never be satisfied. The fear so deeply ingrained in me that I will miss out on something good keeps me chasing after things and exhausting myself as I pursue every good thing in my path. But at some point, I get burnt out and I'm left feeling as if I will never have enough. No matter how hard I try to chase after more, I will always reach a point where I realize it will never satisfy me. It's a ruthless game without a reward.

Even if I had all the things I want in the world, it wouldn't be enough. The only *enough*, the only satisfaction that exists, isn't in a thing but a Person: Jesus.

I will be honest: it can sound too simple to say the solution to constantly consuming new things is finding satisfaction in Jesus. It's easy to say, "Be fully satisfied in Jesus," but it's an entirely different thing to actually do it.

Be patient with yourself on the journey. It's not like flipping on a light switch. More than likely, you will be constantly fighting the lies in your mind—that somehow, the things of this world will satiate you—with the truth of God's Word that only He can give you the complete satisfaction for which you long. To fight lies with the truth, you have to know the difference. You have to know the truth, be able to repeat it to yourself, and proclaim it over yourself. You have to know the lies and be able to cut them off before they become deeply rooted.

Here are some truths about who God is to remind yourself that He alone can fulfill you:

> God is good. God is loving. God is kind. God will provide abundantly for you. God can provide for all of your needs. God is in control. God is with you. God will take care of you. God made you. God knows you. God sees you. God loves you!

How do we find sobriety and satisfaction in God? I think it begins by quietly reflecting on who He is. Then it becomes easier to clear the lies from our minds and replace them with the truth and the One who supplies that truth. When I reflect on my heavenly Father, my earthly desires seem to melt away. I find confidence in my Lord, who is taking care of me and fills me with His love and everything that I truly need.

Fixing my eyes on God, I praise Him for the things that bring me joy and comfort as gifts from Him, not things to be worshipped in and of themselves.

SHIFT IN FOCUS

Write a letter to yourself. Begin with an honest list of things that you want or believe you need in order to be satisfied. Then, write truths about who God is and who you are in Him. Remind yourself of these truths, cling to them, and be gentle with yourself as you shift your mind to recognizing that God is in control, that all good things come from Him, and only He can satisfy.

10 DAYS OF LONG-SUFFERING
Your Strength and How to Use It

What Is Long-Suffering?

*Not only that, but we rejoice in our sufferings, knowing that
suffering produces endurance, and endurance produces character,
and character produces hope.*
(Romans 5:3–4)

Long-suffering is one way that Sevens reflect the character of
God. This trait is quieter than the others you reflect, such as
joy and hope, but it is altogether beautiful to observe. It's not
often that one hears long-suffering mentioned in connection
with Sevens—influencers are more likely to post memes about
Sevens buying a ticket for yet another last-minute vacation—but
those of us who know and love Sevens can attest to the truth of
long-suffering in their lives.

But what is long-suffering? It means having or showing
patience in spite of troubles, especially those caused by other
people.

Long-suffering means getting all of the facts before reacting
negatively, being strong so others can fall apart, and doing the
next right thing. In essence, *long-suffering is the action of patience.*

We often think of patience as playing a sitting and waiting
game, one you may personally abhor. But true long-suffering is
patience in action. It means choosing not to react, choosing to
turn the other cheek, choosing to rejoice in suffering, choosing
to be the comforter instead of one demanding comfort, choosing
to be strong in the face of trial, choosing to look on the bright

side, and choosing to cheer up others instead of giving in to despair. Patience and long-suffering go hand in hand; you cannot be long-suffering without having patience when your actions are hitting some unseen target.

Long-suffering is a compassionate response, a selfless gift to others. It's a beautiful gift of type Sevens.

SHIFT IN FOCUS

When you read the definition of long-suffering, can you identify it in your own life relatively quickly?

Take some time to pray and think through the times that you have sacrificed your own right to *react* for the good of others. How have these situations affected you?

• • • • • • • • • • • DAY 22

How Am I Long-Suffering?

With all humility and gentleness, with patience,
bearing with one another in love.
(Ephesians 4:2)

Dear Seven, there is so much more to you than the fun, joyful, and energetic person the world sees. Sevens are deep, loving, and very intelligent people. If you've ever questioned whether you are indeed a Seven because you're not happy all the time, you're a deep thinker, or you're just an emotional person, I want to reassure you that you're in the right place.

The stereotyping and misconceptions surrounding Sevens can be very hurtful and damaging to them; such concepts can also negatively impact the way others perceive Sevens. I want to apologize on behalf of my fellow Enneagram teachers for this. The preconceived idea that Sevens are merely fun, enthusiastic, whimsical people is one of the reasons you don't often hear about long-suffering as connected to Sevens. However, this aspect of your personality is definitely something that should be talked about more often as it is one of the beautiful ways you show the rest of us the character of Christ.

Sevens act on long-suffering by turning the other cheek, forgiving, being patient with people, and offering second chances. They often remain strong so that others can fall apart.

Long-suffering is a self-sacrificing practice that doesn't give in to the emotion of the moment, but chooses grace and waits to mourn, become angry, or otherwise react. Sevens are often the glue that holds a family together. While they can be counted on to entertain, a lot of families also rely on Sevens to be the strong ones in trials and grief.

Whether this is your family story or not, I'm sure there have been multiple occasions for you to practice long-suffering, and you are very familiar with its joys and its cost.

SHIFT IN FOCUS

What is something you wish others understood about Sevens? Message an account you follow and share this information about your number. They will probably relish your feedback! As someone who hosts a pretty big Instagram page, I know that I jump at any chance to learn about an Enneagram type from that type.

How can you see long-suffering as a trait of God? Where in your life recently has God been actively patient with you?

• • • • • • • • • • • **DAY 23**

Long-Suffering and Joy
By Molly Wilcox

And so, from the day we heard, we have not ceased to pray for you,
asking that you may be filled with the knowledge of his will…bearing
fruit in every good work and increasing in the knowledge of God;
being strengthened with all power, according to his glorious might, for
all endurance and patience with joy; giving thanks to the Father, who
has qualified you to share in the inheritance of the saints in light.
(Colossians 1:9–12)

I don't generally consider myself to be a patient person. I don't really like to wait for things and *delayed gratification* has never made a lot of sense to me. If something is good, new, or exciting, I want it now—please! But sometimes, I think waiting can actually be rewarding and fun. For example, I've always had a blast while standing in long lines. I know this may sound crazy, but a Black Friday sale? Bring it on!

I love the feeling of anticipation building while I wait in line at an amusement park. I may even have more fun in line than I actually do on the ride itself. Thinking about the thrills to come, talking with the people around me, and feeling giddy with excitement while I wait is one of the best experiences. I actually think God has gifted us, as Sevens, with this sense of joy and hope in the waiting, for ourselves and the world around us, when things are hard.

Long-suffering is essentially endurance. When people in my life are waiting to hear back about a job opportunity, waiting to get an offer on their home, or waiting for God to show up, I want to know about it and I want to wait with them. I want to wait and endure with patience and joy. I will be on the phone praying and proclaiming God's promises over them because the future I see, before it becomes a reality, is full of God's joy...and it's worth the wait.

I know that for many people, it can feel challenging and painful to sit in a season of waiting. For them, it's uncomfortable because there's uncertainty looming around the corner.

But I desire to take that opportunity to show the world how waiting for God to move can be like waiting in line at an amusement park. We can enjoy each other's company; we can enjoy the experience of knowing who our Father is and knowing the promise that lies ahead of us after we wait. Psalm 27:14 tells us, *"Wait for the LORD!"* Even when we don't know how long the wait is, we know who is there, and I want to find and reflect joy in the waiting.

SHIFT IN FOCUS

Think of someone in your life who is facing a season of waiting. Ask God to show you how he or she can endure this season with joy and patience, and ask God to use you as a source of encouragement in this person's life. You may even want to schedule a time to have coffee with that person. You could be a source of joy to them while they wait.

• • • • • • • • • • • DAY 24

What Does God Say About Long-Suffering?

Therefore, since we have been justified by faith, we have peace with God through our Lord Jesus Christ. Through him we have also obtained access by faith into this grace in which we stand, and we rejoice in hope of the glory of God. Not only that, but we rejoice in our sufferings, knowing that suffering produces endurance, and endurance produces character, and character produces hope, and hope does not put us to shame, because God's love has been poured into our hearts through the Holy Spirit who has been given to us.
(Romans 5:1–5)

Depending on which translation of the Bible you have, you may not see *long-suffering* in God's Word. Although it appears in the King James Version of the Bible, most other translations use the word *patience* instead. Although the words are closely related, the English word *patience* has a broader meaning than *long-suffering*, which refers to an action-oriented endurance, or patience in suffering.

The verse from the letter to the Romans suggests that followers of Jesus *"rejoice in our sufferings,"* which can seem like an odd concept. If something horrible is happening, why would we rejoice?

However, as a Seven, I'm sure you have witnessed that there is always a reason for rejoicing, even in the midst of great pain. This kind of rejoicing produces endurance, or long-suffering. It's the strength you need to get through trials and the patience to proceed in a godly way.

The Holy Spirit helps us with this type of long-suffering, which is pleasing to God. If you look at Jesus's ministry on earth, and how the Holy Spirit helped Him with long-suffering, you can see how important this gift is and how generous God is when He pours it out onto His children.

The Bible does not promise an easy life for believers; in fact, Jesus said, *"In the world you will have tribulation"* (John 16:33). Trials and suffering are part of our earthly life.

But the fruit of *long-suffering* poured out onto us by the Holy Spirit is part of the grand narrative of God's people clinging to the hope of eternal life with Him.

SHIFT IN FOCUS

Reread Romans 5:1–5. Notice the steps on the path to hope:

Peace > Faith > Rejoicing > Endurance > Character > Hope

Which step on this path do you struggle with the most? Which step is easiest for you?

If you are struggling with one particular step on this path to an eternal hope, then take a moment to ask God to help you. The good news is, God is not asking us to take any of these steps on our own. He is with us and helping us every step of the way.

• • • • • • • • • • • **DAY 25**

Long-Suffering and Paul

Now I rejoice in my sufferings for your sake, and in my flesh I am filling up what is lacking in Christ's afflictions for the sake of his body, that is, the church.
(Colossians 1:24)

If anyone had a reason to boast of suffering, it was the apostle Paul. He was beaten, hated, imprisoned, betrayed, shipwrecked, starved, and separated from the people he loved. Paul even mentions *"a thorn was given me in the flesh"* (2 Corinthians 12:7), but whether this was an actual thorn, a disease, or a sin he could never overcome, we don't know. Whatever it was, it was a burden to him nonetheless.

All of this happened to Paul because he was called to share the gospel to the ends of the earth. He faced spiritual and earthly attacks with hope and purpose, refusing to let anything stop him from his mission. Paul was dedicated to the early church and the new Christians of his day because of his love for Christ. He wanted everyone to live out the hope that he had and experience the love of our Savior.

In his letter to the Colossians, Paul mentions that he rejoices in the suffering he experiences because it enables him to take up his own cross and follow Jesus's example in the battle against sin and death.

Then Jesus told his disciples, "If anyone would come after me, let him deny himself and take up his cross and follow me. For whoever would save his life will lose it, but whoever loses his life for my sake will find it. (Matthew 16:24–25)

Paul truly embraced these sentiments expressed by the apostle Peter:

Do not be surprised at the fiery trial when it comes upon you to test you, as though something strange were happening to you. But rejoice insofar as you share Christ's sufferings, that you may also rejoice and be glad when his glory is revealed.
(1 Peter 4:12–13)

Paul endured suffering for us, the church, and devoted his life to spreading the good news of Jesus Christ.

SHIFT IN FOCUS

You may not be experiencing the extremes of suffering for Christ as Paul did, but can you relate to the idea of patiently enduring for the sake of someone else—perhaps your family, friends, or as an example for your fellow Christians? Do you look for a reason to rejoice in suffering to show others the hope of Christ?

In these ways, like Paul, your brother in Christ, you're taking up your cross and dying to yourself so that others may witness your hope in Jesus.

What are some examples of long-suffering for others in your life?

• • • • • • • • • • • DAY 26

When Long-Suffering Is Godly
By Molly Wilcox

Being strengthened with all power, according to his glorious might,
for all endurance and patience with joy.
(Colossians 1:11)

When I was younger, my mom would compare me and my sisters to different types of flowers. She said I was her sunflower because I was always bright and happy and could grow anywhere. I don't think she worried about me very much, simply because she saw that no matter the circumstances, I was able to put on a smile and grow through it.

The ability to endure through difficult times and continue to grow despite seasons of suffering can be a good and godly thing. Scripture tells us *"suffering produces endurance, and endurance produces character, and character produces hope"* (Romans 5:3–4).

With Jesus, no matter how vast or hard the suffering may seem, we will always have hope in our Savior, in His Holy Spirit who lives in us, and in our place in His kingdom.

Long-suffering can reflect the power of the Holy Spirit to a world in need. As we are able to endure difficult circumstances in life, it becomes clear to those around us that we could not endure in our own strength. It becomes clear there is a great power at work, a power found in the person of Jesus. Our hope is bigger than things that may shake up our current world because of the promises and hope we have in eternity.

Enduring with the help of the Holy Spirit gives the world a reflection of how a relationship with Him changes and shifts our ability to live in this present world. Long-suffering can tell the world the story of the source of hope.

Like a sunflower, I hope you grow brightly despite whatever dirt you may find yourself in today. I hope you reflect the hope we have to a world who desperately needs Him. Through your ability to continue and persist despite challenges, you can usher hope into your community.

SHIFT IN FOCUS

Journal about a time when you or your community faced a season of suffering.

Were you able to *rejoice* in the suffering and endure by the power of the Holy Spirit?

How can God help to bring hope through endurance?

How have you seen this in your life?

• • • • • • • • • • • DAY 27

How Long-Suffering Loves Others

Do nothing from selfish ambition or conceit, but in humility count others more significant than yourselves. Let each of you look not only to his own interests, but also to the interests of others.
(Philippians 2:3–4)

Dear Seven, I have no doubt that people mean a lot to you. Sevens are known for surrounding themselves with people; their social lives play center stage in their week, and they tend to attract friends the way bees are drawn to flowers. Enneagram teachers can go on and on about how Sevens are fun, social people...but there's an aspect of Sevens that doesn't get mentioned very often.

You genuinely care about people. You want those around you to have fun, be happy, and experience life to the fullest, just like you try to do. This type of love and concern quickly turns to protection when problems arise.

Long-suffering is loving when you lay aside what you want or feel to serve those around you. You may subconsciously do this, but after time, it becomes a choice. You stay by people's sides when your emotions make you want to hide. You comfort, calm, and distract others, even when you too are hurting.

In this way, you are truly considering the interests of others as more important than your own. This godly, biblical love is a gift.

Now, there are times when you may be tempted to place others' interests ahead of your own, to your own detriment, but we'll talk more about that tomorrow. For today, I want you to be encouraged in this gift and see it as a strength that does not come easily to many people.

As a Seven, people aren't drawn to you simply because they want to have a good time, even if they know that will be the case. Instead, others know that Sevens, especially healthy Sevens, are there for them through any storm.

This kind of friendship is a gift. I know I can speak for your friends and family when I say, "Thank you for the gift of your friendship!"

SHIFT IN FOCUS

When you use long-suffering to help others, you *stay strong so the rest of us can fall apart.*

How has choosing sacrificial love in the face of your own wants, discomfort, and feelings benefitted the relationships you care about the most?

Can you think of a time that God has helped you to put others before yourself?

● ● ● ● ● ● ● ● ● ● ● ● **DAY 28**

When Long-Suffering Is Numbing

Blessed are those who mourn, for they shall be comforted.
(Matthew 5:4)

In one of Jesus's famous Beatitudes from His Sermon on the Mount, Jesus says something that would be confirmed by modern medicine many years later: *"Blessed are those who mourn, for they shall be comforted."*

Any counselor or psychiatrist will tell you that it is healthy to experience grief. Letting ourselves grieve is even beneficial to our health because repressing this deep, heartfelt sorrow can lead to physical and mental ailments, including hair loss, insomnia, skin blemishes, depression, and irritability. When we refuse to grieve, we can find ourselves overwhelmed by everyday tasks and unable to find joy in activities that would normally delight us.

Dear Seven, sometimes long-suffering is a cover-up for the pain you are avoiding. This long-suffering is not aimed at helping others. It's not a witness of hope and it's not healthy; it's simply a way to numb yourself to your problem. When something devastating happens, it's okay to check to make sure everyone else is fine, but you *cannot* forget about yourself.

You don't need to fall apart in front of a crowd, but you do need to assess the damage this situation has done to your own heart so that you too can start healing. Your heart cannot start to fully heal until you take the shrapnel out, but how do you do that?

+ First, you need to acknowledge that the shrapnel is there. Admit to yourself and others, "I'm not okay."

+ Acknowledge the pain you're in by acknowledging, "This hurt me too."

+ Process that pain by crying, journaling, praying, confiding in a friend, counseling, or taking any other step that will help you deal with it in a positive way.

+ Bring your heart to God for healing. Let Him know, "God, I don't know why this happened, but I do know that I am in pain and I need Your healing."

+ Repeat these steps as needed.

The hardest part about any healing is that it does not happen quickly. You can't expect to fully heal from trauma or pain by taking a fifteen-minute break. You need to continually acknowledge, process, and surrender, *over and over again*. One day, you might find that your heart doesn't hurt from that wound anymore, but this is no guarantee that it will not resurface.

Some healing is a process that is only completed in heaven. Isn't it wonderful to realize that there will be full healing for all of us some day? In heaven with our precious Lord, there will be no more tears, pain, or death.

> *He will wipe away every tear from their eyes, and death shall be no more, neither shall there be mourning, nor crying, nor pain anymore, for the former things have passed away.*
> (Revelation 21:4)

SHIFT IN FOCUS

Spend a couple of moments in silence and ask God to assess your heart and heal any damage there.

What has damaged your heart that you often pretend doesn't exist or try to ignore? This could be many things, but if that's too overwhelming, try to pick just one.

DAY 29 • • • • • • • • • • •

When Long-Suffering Is Hurting You

Rather, speaking the truth in love, we are to grow up in
every way into him who is the head, into Christ,
from whom the whole body, joined and held together
by every joint with which it is equipped, when each
part is working properly, makes the body grow
so that it builds itself up in love.
(Ephesians 4:15–16)

Dear Seven, do you feel pressure to be happy? To not have bad days? To walk into every room with a smile?

Have you experienced people not knowing what to do when you're sad, disappointed, or upset? Do people try to pressure or rush you into becoming your happy, upbeat self again?

Over and over again, Sevens I have known have answered these questions in the affirmative. This is one way that long-suffering may be hurting you. If you're the *strong* one, the person who everyone else leans on, then you *can't* have a bad day. You have to be the one to cheer everyone up; you being anything other than your normally happy self isn't tolerated.

This doesn't merely place an unfair expectation on you, but it's also an unbiblical behavior.

As we can see in the verses from Paul's letter to the church in Ephesus, God wants us to speak the truth in love. This means that lying about your state of being is wrong. We also see that the entire body of Christ is connected, so all of us need to be equipped and functioning properly for the whole church to perform as it should.

This means that your physical and emotional well-being is just as important as everyone else's. Part of that well-being is feeling safe to express yourself. You have the freedom to have bad days and the freedom to not carry the weight of others' expectations of you. You are not responsible for lifting their mood when you have your own issues.

The pressure to always be happy is not a weight that you can carry or were ever meant to bear. This pressure can make you repress healthy emotions. It will make you hide and isolate when you can't be yourself. And it can make you start to resent those who expect so much from you.

Instead, you need to speak the truth in love to others. Be honest about where you're at emotionally and what you're struggling with. As the body of Christ, all of us—not just Sevens—are called to bear each other's burdens. Those around you should pray, check in with you, and otherwise be there for you no matter what your mood.

SHIFT IN FOCUS

Have you been hurt by others' expectations of your long-suffering?

What does speaking the truth in love look like for you today?

When you feel like your feelings, wants, or difficulties are too much for others, open your Bible to the Psalms. God cared so much about us processing and experiencing all of the emotions of life that He gave us a whole book to show us a picture of what it can look like to grieve, be angry, rejoice, and praise Him in a godly way.

• • • • • • • • • • • DAY 30

Godly Suffering
By Molly Wilcox

Share in suffering as a good soldier of Christ Jesus.
No soldier gets entangled in civilian pursuits,
since his aim is to please the one who enlisted him.
(2 Timothy 2:3–4)

Suffering isn't a fun or exciting thing to talk about, but it's something we all experience as humans and something we know well as believers in Jesus. Suffering is a reality we face living in a fallen world.

However, I like to look at suffering from a kingdom perspective. We know the war is already won, so we can face trials and tribulations from the knowledge of victory.

Sometimes I like to talk myself through the worst-case scenario. When I am feeling anxious or afraid, it often helps me to get to a place where I literally have to think to myself, *Worst-case scenario, I die. But then I'm with Jesus, worshipping Him forever.*

Suffering feels difficult when I have both feet on the ground and I'm looking down at them. It feels impossible when I am thinking about all of the troubling and hard things that are tangible right in the world around me.

But when I shift my eyes to heaven, I remember why I'm here. I can suffer for a short time here on earth to be with my Father in heaven for all of eternity. I can suffer, knowing my future is secure in heaven. With that mindset, the harsh realities of the world around me become more manageable. I am able to see things through my Father's eyes and my focus becomes clear. I can walk into difficult seasons with boldness, bravery, and confidence. I know I am equipped with the armor of God, I know I have the Holy Spirit, and I know that no matter how difficult today might be, in light of eternity, today is small. With God, suffering does not seem so overwhelming, and the kingdom of heaven starts to invade the earth.

SHIFT IN FOCUS

Take a few moments to meditate on Jesus's death and resurrection and how it has personally impacted you. Then, spend some time in prayer, thanking God for sending His Son to give you eternal life. Ask the Holy Spirit to be with you and equip you today for any suffering you may face personally, in your community, or in the world. Thank Him for His presence.

10 DAYS OF SPINNING

Help with a Neutral Tool

What Is Spinning?

*And we know that for those who love God all things work together
for good, for those who are called according to his purpose.*
(Romans 8:28)

S*pinning* is a tactic that Sevens use in order to not fully feel
pain, discomfort, disappointment, anxiety, or grief. You may
have heard this called optimism or *looking on the bright side*, but
in reality, it's much more than that.

Spinning is what happens in your mind when something
really bad or disappointing happens. Your mind naturally wants
to find some way to lessen the disappointment, so it will try to
focus on something positive. Sometimes, this is a gift to yourself
and those around you; at other times, it's a defense mechanism
that is repressing hard truths.

I once had a Seven client tell me that she drove her children
to the zoo one day only to find it was closed. The drive had been
long, the kids were grumpy, and everyone was disappointed,
including this Seven mom. However, her mind didn't let her stay
in that forlorn state for long. She thought, *Well, it was a beautiful
day for a drive and I'm so glad we got out of the house. Now we can go
to that ice cream parlor on this side of town for a fun treat!* She used
spinning to turn a disappointing day into a pleasant one.

At its best, spinning assures us of the truth that God will
work everything together for good. We can rejoice in the knowledge that He is in control.

Spinning is a neutral tool, which means you get to decide how to use it. I hope these next days will encourage you to use spinning as a gift and help you to discern when it shouldn't be used at all.

SHIFT IN FOCUS

Is spinning something you've recognized in your own life before?

What do you tend to call it?

Has anyone ever called you out for spinning, perhaps telling you that you always seem to look on the bright side?

• • • • • • • • • • • DAY 32

Why Do I Do This?
By Molly Wilcox

So also you have sorrow now, but I will see you again,
and your hearts will rejoice, and no one will take your joy from you.
(John 16:22)

We are living in a time of both joy and sorrow, the promise of heaven and our current life on earth, the already and the *not yet*. We believe Jesus will return, bringing total restoration and full joy, yet our day-to-day existence can still hurt.

Life seems unfair when someone we love gets sick, we lose a job, or we're just dealing with daily disappointments. But we Sevens in particular also feel a deep sense of hope and joy for the future—and so we spin.

Spinning often comes so naturally to me that my negative emotions, hurt, and pain turn into hope for the future and a joyful response. I take disappointment and immediately begin to tell myself a powerful story of the joys ahead. Honestly, I don't want to live in the hurt for long, so I tell myself of the hopeful endings I can anticipate instead of being caught up in the heart-breaking tension of the unknown. At times, this is a good thing. I tell myself of the hope I see through the brokenness in the world and I feel joy despite my circumstances.

Sometimes, however, I need to press pause in the moment of disappointment and admit to myself and to God that there is a disappointment here. I need to acknowledge that it's okay to feel its full weight.

My relationship with God is only true and honest when I allow myself to feel all of my emotions and allow Him to enter in and heal the hurt.

Dear Seven, I want you to cope and I want you to move forward from your pain, but I also want you to know your Father's heart. He is right there with you. When you're hurting, feel His healing presence. Know the goodness of rejoicing on the other side of sorrow.

I'll be honest, spinning a negative situation immediately into something positive is an innate trait for Sevens. I'm quick to proclaim *the bright side* and often it's a strength. But don't miss an opportunity to let God into the darker moments too because in those moments, He is still present and He is still good.

SHIFT IN FOCUS

Look back on the past few weeks or months and think of a situation you immediately spun into a positive. Think about the emotions you felt—perhaps anger, hurt, disappointment, or shame. Where was God in that? How can you invite His presence into that space?

Do you see value in stillness when you experience negative emotions?

Ask the Holy Spirit to guide you in this area and highlight opportunities to grow closer to Him in the coming weeks.

● ● ● ● ● ● ● ● ● ● ● **DAY 33**

A Childhood of Spinning

Even a child makes himself known by his acts,
by whether his conduct is pure and upright.
(Proverbs 20:11)

Spinning usually starts in early childhood, so you may not remember a time when spinning wasn't a natural reaction to disappointment and pain.

As a child, you probably were the happiest when your parents were happy. This is natural for kids, as parents tend to set the mood for the rest of the family. However, young Sevens usually discover that there is something *they* can do to impact their home environment, even if it's just for themselves.

For a child, spinning can include turning a mistake into a joke, breaking an awkward silence, singing in a silly voice, making paper chains while anticipating the next fun thing to do, watching a lot of TV to drown out arguments, or maybe thinking about the ice cream that's been promised for dessert. These are among the ways that Sevens cope with uncertainty, disappointment, and things they cannot control in childhood.

When you used spinning as a child, you discovered things you *could* control and parented yourself in this way. You needed a stable, happy environment, so you often created it in your own head. Most adults try hard to be good parents, but life is fickle. When they are dealing with stressful things, it's difficult for adults to remember what it's like to be a kid. But thankfully, you had yourself and your early beginning in spinning to get you through your most disappointing days as a child.

In Proverbs, we see that even children are known by their deeds. Maybe a childhood of spinning is one of the reasons you knew you were a Seven. Maybe you knew you were considered a happy child, or felt the pressure early on to be upbeat, happy, or a crowd-pleaser.

Recognizing the ways spinning as a child both helped you survive and hindered processing what was really happening is crucial to your growth as a Seven, no matter how much the idea of pondering this heavy topic might make you squirm. Just know that spinning it can be both useful and a tactic to avoid something you should confront. You can have both a happy childhood and a need to process the scars it left you with today. You can have both a difficult childhood and be grateful for the ways God has redeemed your story.

SHIFT IN FOCUS

Can you clearly see the way you used spinning as a child?

Do you harbor some resentment toward your parents for the ways you had to parent yourself? If yes, how do you think this impacts your relationship with them now?

• • • • • • • • • • • DAY 34

The Disappointing Adulthood

> *Now the Lord is the Spirit, and where the*
> *Spirit of the Lord is, there is freedom.*
> (2 Corinthians 3:17)

As a child, adulthood looks like *the life*. You get to eat whatever you want, go wherever you want, buy whatever you want, and stay out or be home whenever you please. Yes, there were so many things that made us long to become grownups, but they could all be summed up as one thing: freedom. As children, we all longed for freedom.

However, when you became an adult—perhaps when you got your driver's license or first real job—you discovered that adulthood is not as freeing as you had assumed.

Yes, you can eat whatever you want, but your body will wear the effects of your food choices.

Yes, you can go wherever you want, but going places near and far can all cost money.

Yes, you can buy what you want, but you *always* have to pay for it eventually.

Yes, you can stay out late, but only if you're off from work that night or get enough sleep for the next day…because work will control more than its fair share of your time.

It's disappointing when you realize that freedom is never truly as attainable as it might seem to be in childhood. Maybe you're hoping that freedom is still somewhere around the corner. Or maybe you're still feeling that sense of disappointment, leading you to cope by spinning your current situation into a positive one.

The good news is that your desire for true freedom is a godly desire. We are meant to be free and not under slavery to sin or this world. Your longing for freedom is actually a longing for your eternal home and a right relationship with God.

SHIFT IN FOCUS

Have you ever thought of your desire for freedom as a longing for heaven?

What was your biggest assumption or anticipation about adulthood that flopped when you finally reached it?

● ● ● ● ● ● ● ● ● ● ● ● **DAY 35**

When Spinning Helps

Count it all joy, my brothers, when you meet trials of various kinds.
(James 1:2)

Spinning can be a God-given gift to Sevens because of how helpful this tool can be when used for His glory and others' good. Here are four ways that spinning can be helpful:

SPINNING HELPS OTHERS

The ability to perceive the good in almost any situation, turn disappointment into an opportunity, or help another see a more hopeful perspective is truly a way that you bless those around you. What comes naturally for you in this area is not something that everyone else is gifted in—not in the slightest. This makes it a gift that you get to use to help others.

SPINNING PREPARES YOU FOR TRIALS

We know that just because spinning is a gift doesn't mean you don't have to do the hard work to *"count it all joy"* when things are looking grim. However, your everyday spinning can turn into disciplined, obedient joy when the time comes. Making spinning a helpful tool in both everyday life as well as preparation for trials. Looking for the good will ultimately remind you that with God, there is always something for which to be thankful and we are not to lose hope.

SPINNING KEEPS YOU CALM IN A CRISIS

While the rest of us might be panicking, you're probably actively spinning the situation or waiting for it to play out before reacting. This keeps you both level-headed in times of crisis and hopeful for a good outcome.

SPINNING GIVES YOU HOPE FOR THE FUTURE

Because spinning gives you hope for the future, Sevens are known for planning, having an entrepreneurial spirit, being multi-passionate, and taking risks. You live under the assumption that everything can turn out okay and probably will. Dear Seven, you get to experience much more of the world and also make a healthy number of mistakes when you trust that mistakes don't define or destroy you. This is a freedom that not many people have and it's a way that spinning truly does help you.

SHIFT IN FOCUS

Can you think of a couple more ways that spinning helps you?

Spend some time in prayer thanking God for this gift and asking Him to help you use it for good.

• • • • • • • • • • • • DAY 36

When Spinning Hinders

> *There is a way that seems right to a man,*
> *but its end is the way to death.*
> (Proverbs 14:12)

Like anything about our Enneagram type, the good aspects of our personality can also be an obstacle to our growth. Even our gifts, talents, and the ways we reflect God are tainted by sin and our own selfish ambition. For Sevens, spinning is a gift, but when sin gets involved, it quickly turns into a hindrance.

It's important to acknowledge this propensity so that you can be on guard toward your own heart and move toward discipline in this area. It is wrong to think that spinning is only good or only bad because it can be both at the same time.

Spinning hinders when you use it to:

+ Excuse or downplay sin

+ Justify your overindulgence or bad choices

+ Dismiss or ignore others' pain because it makes you uncomfortable

+ Ignore serious problems in your life, such as addiction or abuse

+ Distract yourself from the seriousness of your reality by numbing or avoiding issues or situations that should be addressed

If you're in a stressful season and veering toward unhealthy behaviors and attitudes, these hindrances are likely to be within your grasp, or perhaps your present reality. This can be hard to notice, acknowledge, or change because it will be easy to spin your bad behaviors and negative coping mechanisms into, "It's not a big deal," or "This is just who I am." This is where spinning can even become dangerous. Not everything will turn out okay; your choices have consequences, both earthly and eternal.

At the moment of action or temptation, sin can feel and seem right, even good. But Proverbs 14:12 gives us the stern warning not to rely on our own idea, view, or feeling of what is right, but instead lean on God for understanding.

SHIFT IN FOCUS

Spend some time reflecting and praying through these questions:

+ Am I currently using spinning in a way that is hindering my relationship with God?

+ Have I ever used spinning as a hindrance in the past?

+ Are these things I've just moved past without repentance?

• • • • • • • • • • • • DAY 37

Identifying Where Your Spinning Lands
By Molly Wilcox

So we do not lose heart. Though our outer self is wasting away, our inner self is being renewed day by day. For this light momentary affliction is preparing for us an eternal weight of glory beyond all comparison, as we look not to the things that are seen but to the things that are unseen. For the things that are seen are transient, but the things that are unseen are eternal.
(2 Corinthians 4:16–18)

As newlyweds, my husband and I prepared to move across the country to Colorado to start our life together. When we returned from our honeymoon, we drove to our wedding venue to pick up the decorations.

That's when the brakes went out in our car. We managed to roll it to a stop in a parking lot and for a moment, we just sat there, realizing the car we were planning to drive to Colorado had just broken down.

Seeing my husband's panicked and uncertain expression, I immediately started to talk about how great this situation was. He seemed to disagree pretty quickly. After working out the details and dealing with the logistics, we made our move to Colorado as planned...and spent the summer riding bikes to work.

I look back on that summer as a time when we lived simply, spent more time outdoors, and enjoyed being in the heart of our community.

As I reflect, I see both the good and the bad in my tendency to put a positive spin on things. There absolutely was a bright side to the unexpected difficulty we faced—we lived in a little mountain town and biked everywhere for a summer. It was a blast! I still talk about it all the time.

Our car also broke down unexpectedly and it was basically worth nothing. Yet I didn't allow my husband or myself to be discouraged for longer than a moment.

The problem is, when I numb myself to negative emotions—and attempt to do the same thing for the people around me—I actually start to chip away at the opportunity to experience the fullness of the joy of restoration later.

Dear Seven, as you evaluate how you put a positive spin on life, know that it isn't always good and it isn't always bad. The Holy Spirit will illuminate where He is in situations and He can give you an eternal perspective on the world around us. He can show us how we are putting a positive spin on circumstances. In our relationships, this can bring hope and restoration, but we also want to be near to those who are mourning like Jesus was. (See John 11:33–44.) We can't take away all of the disappointments the people around us and we ourselves will experience in life.

SHIFT IN FOCUS

Through honest reflection, allow the Holy Spirit to help you identify where you are spinning situations in your life and in your relationships. Ask God to be your vision and allow you to have an eternal focus.

• • • • • • • • • • • • **DAY 38**

Spinning vs. Choosing Joy
By Molly Wilcox

The light shines in the darkness,
and the darkness has not overcome it.
(John 1:5)

Dear Seven, I do believe spinning can be an appropriate and effective tool to cope with the everyday pains and disappointments we face in the world, but we do need to be careful as we use it. The world can be a dark and difficult place, and the circumstances we face can be foreboding. It can feel like we are walking through the valley of death, even when we know that joy is possible and there is a light that shines in the darkness.

However, we cannot fabricate joy and we cannot spin a negative circumstance into a positive one in our own strength. The light in the darkness is the Lord. He alone is the source of joy; He is the One who brings light to a dark world. I know God can use Sevens to share His light. Jesus said:

> *You are the light of the world....Let your light shine before*
> *others, so that they may see your good works and give glory*
> *to your Father who is in heaven.* (Matthew 5:14, 16)

Don't try to force positivity onto a circumstance, a difficult time, or the people around you. There is a difference between walking through a difficult season with clenched fists and a forced smile and walking through it with your eyes lifted to Jesus, *"the light of the world"* and *"the light of life"* (John 8:12).

I want to walk through dark seasons certain of the light that I can see in the midst of it, knowing that God is the same yesterday, today, and forever. (See Hebrews 13:8.) I want to sense the presence of Jesus, the Prince of Peace. I want to know that the darkness has not and will not overcome. I want to choose joy in every circumstance, but I don't want to put a positive spin on the world in a way that makes it hurt more.

Darkness is a reality of the world we live in, a reality that we face daily as believers. But we don't face it alone and we will not be overcome—that is God's promise. Let's challenge each other to look to the light of the world in the middle of the darkness and not rely on ourselves to bring false positivity when we can rely on our very real and powerful Creator.

SHIFT IN FOCUS

Write about the difficulty or disappointment you have recently faced. Where do you see God bringing restoration to that issue? How can you rely on Him to bring light into a dark circumstance?

As you reflect on this, release yourself from the pressure to make the circumstance seem positive in your own strength.

• • • • • • • • • • • DAY 39

Spinning vs. Being Optimistic

Let no corrupting talk come out of your mouths,
but only such as is good for building up, as fits the occasion,
that it may give grace to those who hear.
(Ephesians 4:29)

It's obvious that some people are more optimistic than others. They have a disposition or tendency to look on a more favorable side of events or conditions and expect the best outcome.

This can sound like spinning, but it's not. And the difference between optimism and spinning can cause of a lot of mistyping between Sevens and other optimistic Enneagram types, namely Twos and Nines.

I'd like you to be able to articulate and know what the difference is, both for yourself and for others in your life who may be confused. Sevens who spin are also likely to be optimistic people, but not every optimist spins negative situations into positive ones.

+ Optimism has a hopeful, peaceful, and resigned energy. Spinning has an active, planning, rewriting, and course-correcting energy.

+ Optimism says, "What will be will be." Spinning says, "What will be will be good, even if it kills me."

+ Optimism acknowledges the negative but hopes for the best. Spinning takes the negative, dusts it off, and turns it into an adventure.

Both optimism and spinning look for the positive, hope for the best, and tend to be more naive about potential danger than pessimists. But overall, being an optimistic person is the posture of those of us who believe in Christ. We hope for the future because Jesus *is* our hope and our future. We look for the positive because we know that God is good. We may be naive in ways of evil because we are not immersed in them. All of these outlooks are good and pleasing to God.

SHIFT IN FOCUS

Have you had it pointed out to you that you're optimistic?

In what ways does your faith in Jesus Christ help you cling to optimism?

• • • • • • • • • • • **DAY 40**

Spinning and Identity

I have been crucified with Christ. It is no longer I who live, but Christ who lives in me. And the life I now live in the flesh I live by faith in the Son of God, who loved me and gave himself for me.
(Galatians 2:20)

We've spent a lot of time examining whether or not spinning in and of itself can be done in godliness. By now, I hope you agree that it certainly can be.

However, there is another issue with spinning and godliness that we have yet to examine, and that issue has to do with identity. As a Seven, a good amount of your self-image and identity may be wrapped up in your ability to remain optimistic and not fall apart when things get rough. It's a kind of tough and independent yet approachable attitude.

As we've seen, your long-suffering and spinning tendencies mean that you're a pretty positive person who is good-natured most of the time. These are good attributes and in no way should they be stifled. However, if your identity—your hope, trust, security, and conceptualization of who you are—is wrapped up in being a positive person, then you're going to fail yourself miserably or cause a lot of damage trying to uphold this persona.

+ As a positive person, you may feel enormous pressure to not have bad days.

+ As a high-energy person, you may decide not to show up instead of showing up tired.

- As a happy person, you may not let yourself process pain in order to maintain your illusion of *happiness*.

- As a person who doesn't fall apart, you may never let others get close enough to see how bad you're actually hurting, thus denying them the chance to help bear your burdens.

God says our identity is to be *"in Christ"* (2 Corinthians 5:17; see also Galatians 2:20). Our Lord and Savior securely holds our hope, trust, security, and ideas about who we are.

Who are you? An adopted daughter or son of God, a sinner saved by amazing grace, a temple of the Holy Spirit, and an ambassador for Christ.

This means that your identity is not caught up in something that needs to be done, but in something that has already occurred.

Your identity cannot be altered or destroyed by a bad day or devastating circumstances because *a happy, high energy, positive person* is not who you are. Yes, you tend to be such a person and that's a gift from God, but who you are is a much deeper matter.

Who you are should not be wrapped up in behaviors, circumstances, or what others think of you. Jesus has much more in mind for you than that.

SHIFT IN FOCUS

Do you feel like your identity is wrapped up in being a happy, positive, high-energy person?

If you could no longer be *the happy person* for a season, how would that make you feel?

How would clinging to your identity *"in Christ"* change what you expect from yourself?

10 DAYS OF DEALING WITH PERFECTION

Going to One in Stress

● ● ● ● ● ● ● ● ● ● ● **DAY 41**

Seasons of Life

For everything there is a season, and a time for every matter under heaven: a time to be born, and a time to die; a time to plant, and a time to pluck up what is planted; a time to kill, and a time to heal; a time to break down, and a time to build up; a time to weep, and a time to laugh; a time to mourn, and a time to dance; a time to cast away stones, and a time to gather stones together; a time to embrace, and a time to refrain from embracing; a time to seek, and a time to lose; a time to keep, and a time to cast away; a time to tear, and a time to sew; a time to keep silence, and a time to speak; a time to love, and a time to hate; a time for war, and a time for peace.
(Ecclesiastes 3:1–8)

In the whirlwind of life, expectations, and demands, it can be hard to think of ourselves as living seasonally. We live on an earth with winter, spring, summer, and fall, and we observe and celebrate the earth and its seasons, but we rarely give ourselves permission to change and transform. Instead, we expect all or nothing. Either I am…or I am not. There is *right now*, and anything worth doing is worth doing *today*. This is especially true in the hustle of America.

Of course, as we look at our own life, seasons are evident. There was that really hard year of illness, there were years of singleness, there were those amazing three months of falling in love, there were years with little kids, there were years of learning— everything in its own season.

We have a lot to learn from the way God created the earth with its seasons. In these verses from Ecclesiastes, Solomon notes there is a season for everything, and we can see that he's talking about us, not just the earth. The wisest king who ever lived says that for every bad or hard season we experience, there is a season of rest and good to come.

SHIFT IN FOCUS

In the next nine days, we will go into detail about what seasons of stress look like for you as a Seven.

As you look at your own life today, what season are you in? Read Ecclesiastes 3:1–8 again and pick one or two adjectives that represent the season you're currently in. Are you mourning or celebrating? Transitioning or resting? Uprooting or planting?

If you're in a more hopeful, joyful, and restful season, it may be time to press into growth and celebrate the growth you can see in yourself. If you're in a season of hard transition and survival, it may be helpful for you to view this time as a passing season and discover hope on the horizon. You may see some ways that you're growing even in stress and adversity. Celebrate those wins!

• • • • • • • • • • • DAY 42

Seasons of Stress?

How long must I take counsel in my soul and have sorrow in my heart all the day? How long shall my enemy be exalted over me? Consider and answer me, O LORD my God; light up my eyes, lest I sleep the sleep of death, lest my enemy say, "I have prevailed over him," lest my foes rejoice because I am shaken.
(Psalm 13:2–4)

In light of talking about seasons, I think we all know that there are seasons of stress we walk through. Some are lighter than others, but all bring the anxiety and feeling of trying to survive that's familiar to us all.

When we talk about stress using Enneagram verbiage, we aren't talking about being late for work or losing your keys. Most of us get frustrated and irritable in those circumstances. No, when the Enneagram refers to stress, it means seasonal stress—you just lost your job, you're transitioning, your loved one just passed away, and other harsh or trying circumstances. In those times, you're often in survival mode for months or years.

For an Enneagram Seven, seasons of stress look like picking up the more negative behaviors of a type One. You will not functionally *become* a type One, but your normally fun, hopeful, and friendly disposition can take quite the shift during these seasons.

If you look back on seasons of stress in your life—or if you're in one now—you are likely to see some of these coping behaviors:

- You may start to see flaws around you and it'll become hard to not fixate on them

- You may struggle with critical self-talk

- You may binge clean or organize

- You may fixate on planning something fun for the future to avoid dealing with the stress you're feeling

- You may get irritated with those around you for not helping

- You may snap at people trying to cheer you up

These behaviors, dear Seven, are a huge red flag that you're in a season of stress. Can you feel these in yourself right now? This season, like the ones before it, will pass. But acknowledging the season at hand and giving yourself grace for survival will serve you greatly during what can be a very frustrating time.

SHIFT IN FOCUS

Do you believe you're currently in a season of stress?

What couple of One behaviors do you see most often when you're in seasons of stress?

• • • • • • • • • • • **DAY 43**

Going to One in Stress

> *Peace I leave with you; my peace I give to you.*
> *Not as the world gives do I give to you.*
> *Let not your hearts be troubled, neither let them be afraid.*
> (John 14:27)

In a season of stress, which commonly coincides with a transition, you'll develop coping mechanisms as a way to maintain control. However, what you gain by *going to type One* is a false sense of control or security rather than actually achieving either. These *false control* solutions often look like obsessively cleaning, criticizing yourself or others, or otherwise fixating on things to fix.

A clean kitchen may be something you can control. You might be able to control your weight to some extent. That bedroom mirror that's been crooked for months but never bothered you before is suddenly something you can fix. Planning out a vacation for next year might feel like being in control of something.

All of these coping mechanisms will give you a momentary feeling of being in control, but they don't fix the actual reason you're stressed. No amount of cleaning will make your job environment better, no amount of dieting will make your mom's cancer go away, and no amount of future planning actually removes you from the here and now.

At best, these coping mechanisms are distractions; at their worst, they're keeping you from God's purpose, comfort, and presence here for you right now.

What you really want is for this season to be solved, over, and finished so you can stop feeling the negative emotions and thinking the negative thoughts that are making you angsty and uncomfortable.

SHIFT IN FOCUS

Reread John 14:27.

The world's peace might look like a clean house, a new car, or a future adventure, but your soul is longing for something that will last. We ache for something much bigger than ourselves and what we can control. We ache for the peace that God can give.

Next time you're tempted by your stress-coping mechanisms, ask yourself, "What am I really longing for? Do I believe God can provide this for me or give me peace even if my situation isn't fixed?"

• • • • • • • • • • • **DAY 44**

Stress and Critical Self-Talk
By Molly Wilcox

> *Let no corrupting talk come out of your mouths,*
> *but only such as is good for building up, as fits the occasion,*
> *that it may give grace to those who hear.*
> (Ephesians 4:29)

Dear Seven, sometimes it feels like life doesn't meet our grand and wild expectations. It's stressful and we feel let down by what we wanted life to be like. In our darker moments, in the moments when we feel like we cannot manage and we are unsure of what the future holds, we can be so quick to lift up the people around us while forgetting to speak kindly and positively to ourselves.

When I read the verse from Ephesians, I think I do a good job of "*building up*" those around me. I am a natural encourager and I'm willing to bet you are too. But if I reread that verse and ask myself honestly if it is being upheld in my thought life, the answer is quite different.

Sometimes, I get disappointed or stressed out. My silent response within my mind is to lean into those Enneagram One traits and become critical of myself. Why am I not handling the stress better? Why isn't the world around me meeting my expectations? Why am I not happier? Why do I feel so negative and disappointed inside? Why is it trapped in my mind and why can't I tell someone? Why do I try to tell the world around me everything's okay, when honestly, sometimes I'm not sure it is?

Maybe you have asked yourself one of these questions or something similar. Maybe you too begin to feel misplaced guilt when expectations are low and life isn't as *good* as you desperately want it to be. This is why a lot of Sevens think they have an inner critic like type Ones when they're stressed. In reality, it is really our own thoughts, criticisms, and harsh view of our reactions that we are using as a weapon against ourselves.

The *only* way to get out of this is to give grace to yourself. Let yourself be disappointed, sad, or feeling let down. The world isn't perfect and neither are the people in it. Sometimes, things don't turn out the way you hope they will. But you know who *is* perfect. This is your chance to take control of your thought life and welcome Jesus there.

Christ has already given us an infinite amount of grace, so let's extend it to ourselves. Let's be gentle when we talk to ourselves. Let's let the voice in our head be one that builds up, forgives, speaks kindly, and gives grace in times of stress.

SHIFT IN FOCUS

Take a moment to invite the Holy Spirit to guide you in a time of self-reflection. Think of a negative or harmful thought you have had recently. Invite the Holy Spirit to reveal the truth He believes about you. Ask Him to guide you in forgiving yourself, and extending grace. Ask Him to continually give you His thoughts about you and pray that He will guide you to believe them in stressful times.

• • • • • • • • • • • **DAY 45**

Stress and Binge Cleaning

> *For the LORD sees not as man sees: man looks on the outward*
> *appearance, but the LORD looks on the heart.*
> (1 Samuel 16:7)

When you feel like a mess on the inside, it can be a normal human reaction to try to clean up the outside. I am writing this devotional a couple of months into the COVID-19 pandemic and I'm currently seeing a lot of posts on social media about getting dressed every day, keeping your work-space tidy, and making an effort to exercise and eat well.

What's going on outside, in the world around us, can deeply impact how we feel about ourselves and our mood. This is one of the reasons you may have a fondness toward binge cleaning. After it's done, you may feel lighter internally and without clutter adding to your stress, it can be easier to think and assess what's really going on.

However, we need to be careful of two things here. Make sure you are not:

1. Using cleaning as a form of self-punishment. (Refer to day 46.)

2. Distracting yourself and avoiding self-care that you need.

Sometimes when we are trying to make our appearance, our workplace, or our homes more presentable, it's because we are trying to gain all of those good things I mentioned earlier. We want to feel like less of a mess on the inside, we want to be proud of ourselves, and we want to feel presentable.

However, there are situations in which fixing the mess won't fix what's going on inside. It will only dull the sensation of pain, confusion, or angst you may be feeling. And yes, that may sound like a good thing, but any counselor will tell you, "If something is hurting, it's because it needs to be tended to, not ignored."

That's the whole reason for pain, isn't it? Pain lets us know something is wrong. So if you're consistently distracting and dulling your sensation of internal pain, you're going to end up with a bigger problem. Distracting yourself by binge cleaning is like taking pain medication for a deep wound when what you really need is stitches.

God cares more about what's going on in your heart than how you look on the outside, how clean your house is, or whether that project gets done in a timely manner. He wants to meet you in the inner mess and chaos so He can lead you to lasting growth and change.

That pain that you're trying to dull might just be the very thing that God wants to heal. Although a momentary sense of relief might satisfy you for now, He desires much more for your heart.

SHIFT IN FOCUS

When you're tempted to binge clean or find yourself binge cleaning, ask yourself:

+ What am I stressed about?

+ Is there something I can do about this? (Make a call, pay a bill, have a hard conversation with someone, etc.)

+ If there is nothing you can do, then set a timer for one hour and let yourself clean. Go do your make-up, or put on some nice clothes instead of pajamas. Read your Bible and offer up your situation to God in prayer.

Not all coping is bad, but you need to be aware of your reasons. Do you notice patterns of avoiding, numbing, or distracting? Pray and ask God to remind you in those times to come to His open arms and receive rest.

DAY 46 • • • • • • • • • • • •

But Isn't Cleaning a Good Thing?

All we like sheep have gone astray; we have turned—every one—to his own way; and the LORD *has laid on him the iniquity of us all.* (Isaiah 53:6)

Dear Seven, I can't tell you how many times I've been in coaching sessions with Sevens who have spun their cleaning stress behaviors into something positive. Yes, in itself, cleaning is not bad. In fact, it can make you feel like you've accomplished something and relieve a bit of stress. This is why you may remember your binge cleaning with some amount of pride and fondness.

However, we need to look at this behavior a little more critically. When we do, we see that this sheep may be a wolf in disguise.

When something breaks, there usually is someone to blame, right? Things usually don't fall to pieces on their own. This might be how you're viewing your current stress situation. You may be either blaming yourself for it or blaming yourself for your negative feelings or reaction toward what's happening.

So what do you do? You punish yourself.

Read that again.

You punish yourself for causing yourself pain. You punish yourself for bad choices that might've gotten you here. You punish yourself because you shouldn't be this stressed. You punish yourself because the blame needs to fall on someone—and blaming yourself gives you the most control.

Binge cleaning is often a form of self-punishment for Sevens. It's a physical childhood punishment that doesn't *look* like what it's actually doing to your soul.

Dieting is a form of self-punishment for Sevens.

Restricting *fun* is a form of self-punishment for Sevens.

Not letting yourself enjoy life or grounding yourself is a form of self-punishment for Sevens.

As Christians, Jesus took our punishment upon Himself. We do not need to be punished for anything we have done in the past or may do in the future. Jesus took that punishment for you on the cross.

> *For our sake* [God] *made him to be sin who knew no sin, so that in him we might become the righteousness of God.*
> (2 Corinthians 5:21)

As Christians, we should not be punishing ourselves; when we do, we're in essence saying that Jesus's sacrifice wasn't enough to atone for what we have done. This is not only false, but it's also very damaging to our thoughts about ourselves and God. God's grace is not ours to reject.

Jesus's punishment was enough to cover your mistakes, errors, and sins, today, tomorrow, and forever. Binge cleaning as a form of self-punishment is not something to brush off as *no big deal*.

SHIFT IN FOCUS

Your first thought upon reading the message for this day might be, *But I don't punish myself by cleaning.* However, please sit with this thought and give it some reflection.

Ask yourself if there could be some truth to this in your past season of stress. And if you're in a season of stress now, how can you be kind to yourself in the midst of accomplishing and getting stuff done?

What does kindness to yourself look like right now? Does kindness look like not letting yourself clean after 9 p.m. or maybe only for an hour at a time? Does kindness look like breaking up the workload over a couple of days or delegating it to family members? Does kindness look like letting your space be less than perfect right now and giving yourself grace that that's okay?

The Lord says, *"Vengeance is mine"* (Deuteronomy 32:35). It's not up to us to dole out punishment for others or ourselves.

• • • • • • • • • • DAY 47

Stress and Black or White Thinking

But woe to you, scribes and Pharisees, hypocrites! For you shut the kingdom of heaven in people's faces. For you neither enter yourselves nor allow those who would enter to go in.
(Matthew 23:13)

As seasons of stress become intense, you may be tempted to cling to the security of black or white thinking. Considering rules, order, and right versus wrong can give you a natural sense of security because seeing absolutes means you can control your thoughts and actions accordingly, often escaping further punishment or calamity.

This is how Ones handle the uncertainty of life in general, and it may be a way that you handle the uncertainty of your stress seasons.

For Sevens, this may look like:

+ Trying to find a new diet and style of eating that is *right*

+ Creating rules around entertainment or free time

+ Clinging to political rights or wrongs, or being attracted to very strong opinions

+ Correcting people who think differently than you do, especially online

+ Getting easily discouraged or offended when others don't obey the rules

+ Road rage

+   Budgeting, usually to an extreme

These may all be things you don't normally do, or aren't very attractive to you, but you may start to do them when you're in stress and tempted to indulge in black or white thinking.

Thinking in absolutes may give you a sense of security or control, but it assumes much more than it knows. The outcome of black or white thinking can be burnt bridges, damaged relationships, and even poor health.

In the time of Jesus, the Pharisees clung to rules to give themselves a sense of security. The problem was that they added more rules to their lists than God originally gave them. Jesus was quick to point out the error of their ways and show them that they could not save themselves by following the rules. They needed to realize that they needed a Savior and lay down their self-righteous identities as rule followers because it wasn't doing anything to secure their place in heaven.

Like the Pharisees, you might be clinging to more rules in seasons of stress, but they aren't helping you any more than the Pharisees' rules helped them.

SHIFT IN FOCUS

What type of rules are you tempted to cling tightly to in stress?

Does clinging to these rules make it harder for you to love the people who break them?

In what way does other people's black or white thinking hurt you?

• • • • • • • • • • • DAY 48

Stress and God's Comfort

Even though I walk through the valley of the shadow of death,
I will fear no evil, for you are with me; your rod and your staff,
they comfort me.
(Psalm 23:4)

Psalm 23 is arguably one of the most popular chapters in all of Scripture. Even nonbelievers are familiar with some of these iconic verses. But as familiar as you may be with this psalm, have you ever really thought about that last line in verse 4?

"Your rod and your staff, they comfort me."

If you've ever seen a picture of a shepherd, or you're familiar with farm life, you may have wondered why a shepherd has a rod and a staff.

The shepherd uses the short, club-like rod to protect the sheep against predators and also to direct the sheep. Sometimes, he may even use it as a disciplinary device against the more ornery sheep.

The staff, on the other hand, is a long stick with a crook at the end that the shepherd can use to hook around a sheep's neck and pull it away from danger, such as an area with poisonous plants or a cliff. The shepherd can also use his staff as a walking stick.

These tools of a shepherd were essential to protect the flock and keep the sheep in line. So why does King David, who wrote this psalm, correlate these items to comfort?

Protection, discipline, and rules are all things that we crave as humans, even when we run from them. As an Enneagram Seven going to One in stress, rules can start to feel very safe. Without rules, how do you know what's the right thing to do? Without rules, we would have chaos. This is the spirit of what the psalmist was talking about here.

God's rules are for our protection. Like parents who don't let their children play in the street, God has rules for our safety because He doesn't want us to get hurt. (See the Ten Commandments, Exodus 20:1–17.)

God protects us from our *"adversary the devil [who] prowls around like a roaring lion, seeking someone to devour"* (1 Peter 5:8).

> *But the Lord is faithful. He will establish you and guard you against the evil one.* (2 Thessalonians 3:3)

God's discipline is for our protection, but is also comforting because we know that if we start wandering out of line or get lost from the flock, God's staff is right there ready to lead us back. He may have to pull us out of a thicket by the neck, but He *will* go after us.

> *What do you think? If a man has a hundred sheep, and one of them has gone astray, does he not leave the ninety-nine on the mountains and go in search of the one that went astray?* (Matthew 18:12)

> *My son, do not despise the LORD's discipline or be weary of his reproof, for the LORD reproves him whom he loves, as a father the son in whom he delights.* (Proverbs 3:11–12)

SHIFT IN FOCUS

Reflect on the comfort of God's rules, protection, and discipline. How have these things been a comfort to you in stress?

Do you thank God for His rules, protection, and discipline in your prayers? Spend some time thanking Him for these comforting gifts of love.

DAY 49 • • • • • • • • • • •

Letting Yourself Be Stressed with Grace

But if it is by grace, it is no longer on the basis of works;
otherwise grace would no longer be grace.
(Romans 11:6)

If you are in a season of stress, your first instinct may be to place blame somewhere.

+ "If that driver had been paying attention, I wouldn't have a broken leg."

+ "If the government were competent, minimum wage would be higher and I wouldn't be struggling."

+ "If the doctors had caught Grandma's cancer sooner, she'd still be here."

+ "If I had just prepared better, I wouldn't be stressed now."

+ "If I could just _____ (*fill in the blank*), I wouldn't be stressed."

This is a remnant of your own childhood thinking. The vase shattered and your parent's first question was, "Who broke this?" You are using their example to self-parent—something we all do, by the way—to deal with the harsh realities of adulthood.

The problem is, this logic doesn't transfer to every situation of adulthood as it might in childhood.

In adulthood, there is room for things to be bad, horrible, or broken and still be *no one's fault.* Even if you or someone else is to blame for the season of stress you're in, you need to let God deal with the punishment. God will take care of it, either on the cross of Jesus or in hell; this is His justice.

Seasons of stress should be seasons in which you have radical grace for yourself. *You are surviving.* You can't expect as much out of yourself as you would in a season of growth because you literally will not have as much to give.

Slowing down and giving yourself grace in seasons of stress can look like:

+ Napping instead of working out

+ Taking a bath instead of being productive

+ Cutting back on your commitments

+ Not expecting yourself to perform at 100 percent

+ Saying aloud, "I'm surviving and I get to do that without disappointing myself."

+ Telling yourself, "This season will pass and I will wish I was easier on myself during it."

+ Saying to yourself and others, "Maybe not right now, but later."

SHIFT IN FOCUS

Spend some time in prayer, asking God to search your heart as you answer these questions:

+ Do you struggle with trying to place blame and enforce punishment during seasons of stress?

+ In what way is God inviting you to have grace for yourself during these seasons?

• • • • • • • • • • • **DAY 50**

Going to God in Seasons of Stress
By Molly Wilcox

> *Many are the plans in the mind of a man,*
> *but it is the purpose of the LORD that will stand.*
> (Proverbs 19:21)

When I get stressed out, I'm quick to try to control the situation to the best of my ability. Trying to plan my stress away, I love to make long to-do lists and organize my calendar like a fanatic, complete with color-coded gel pens.

One of the most stressful seasons of my life was getting married just two months after college graduation. I had countless appointments scheduled; I was blocking off time for wedding planning, being with my fiancé, homework, and going to classes.

I mapped out our entire wedding weekend and sent out incredibly detailed, minute-by-minute schedules to everyone. I listed emergency contacts and addresses for every event. I even left room for error on the day of the ceremony—I literally had scheduled times for when things could possibly go wrong. I knew I was prepared for anything. I had planned the stress away and I was certain I was in control.

When my wedding weekend rolled around, all sorts of things happened that were out of my control. A groomsman passed out. The ceremony started late because we couldn't find the rings. My heels got ruined in the mud so I got married in sneakers. As my dad and I started down the aisle, the train of my gown got caught on something, so we just stood there smiling and laughing until someone freed me.

Honestly, it was kind of a mess—but I loved every single part of it.

I walked away married to the love of my life and all the things that went *wrong* became our favorite stories that we retell with fond memories and laughter.

As Sevens, I think we want to plan in order to control a situation when we're stressed. It's easier to map out our way and focus on that than it is to release our plans to the Lord. As much as I'm tempted to plan my way out of stress, God is ultimately in control and He will have His way. I would rather go to Him first and get on board with His plans than try to force my plans on Him.

We know we have a good Father and we know His plans for us are good, even in stressful seasons. As much as I love color-coding my calendar, ultimately, my planning is giving me a false sense of control. God's plans will prevail no matter what. I can trust Him in a stress season just as I can in a growth season.

SHIFT IN FOCUS

Respond in prayer and if these words reflect your heart, please borrow them:

Dear heavenly Father, may You guide me into Your plans in every season. May I trust in Your faithfulness, in Your provision, in Your goodness, and in Your love.

Guide me gently back into Your arms and help me to trust that You are in control. Remind me of Your faithfulness and Your sovereignty when I am tempted to try to control everything myself. Amen.

10 DAYS OF FOCUS

Going to Five in Growth

Seasons of Growth

Every good gift and every perfect gift is from above,
coming down from the Father of lights,
with whom there is no variation or shadow due to change.
(James 1:17)

As we talked about in the beginning of our conversation about stress, thinking of your life in seasonal terms is not only biblical, but it also gives you a lot more grace and hope for your circumstances. Seasons of stress are the opposite of seasons of growth. The latter are periods in your life in which you feel as if you have room to breathe, have more energy, and can focus on spiritual, mental, and physical growth.

Seasons of growth are often blurry or over-romanticized when we look back at our life as a whole. We either can't remember a time in our life that we didn't feel the hum of anxiety and stress, or we can't live fully in the present because no season will ever be as good as it has been in the past.

Both of these thought processes are unfruitful because they're extremes. There is always a mixture of good and bad in every situation; only the details change. This is a result of living in a fallen world. We are living outside of our natural habitat, and it often feels like a paradox of good and bad at the same time.

Now, this doesn't mean that seasons of stress and growth coexist all the time; often, they don't. Circumstances in our lives often tip the scales. Nothing is ever all bad or all good. Working in a toxic environment or the death of a loved one will send us into a season of stress. Likewise, getting our dream job, hitting a sweet spot with parenting, or flourishing in a good friendship can tip the scale to seasons of growth.

You should push yourself during seasons of growth. Have you been wanting to read a certain book or join a Bible study? Do it! Are you thinking about starting a diet or exercising more? Now's the time! We literally have more mental space, more energy, and more bandwidth when we are in seasons of growth.

We can also see a lot of encouraging behaviors pop up. Press into them and build them in a way that they'll stick beyond this season. Create good habits that will serve a future, stressed-out you. Consistent Bible reading is a must for all of life, but especially those hard days when you feel lost.

Growth seasons are the days of digging deep and reaping the rewards. These seasons are a gift from a heavenly Father who loves you and wants to give you good things.

As we see in 1 Peter 4:10, we should be using these seasons of *good gifts* to not only build up our faith, but also to help others. In the next nine days, you'll see how going to Five in growth helps you specifically with this, and how you can push into your growth number in a practical way.

SHIFT IN FOCUS

Are you currently in a season of growth?

Do you have a couple of good seasons in your past that you might be over-romanticizing, or maybe are ungrateful for?

● ● ● ● ● ● ● ● ● ● ● **DAY 52**

The Best of Type Five

A disciple is not above his teacher, but everyone when he is
fully trained will be like his teacher.
(Luke 6:40)

As you encounter growth seasons, it will become easier for you to access some of the best qualities of Enneagram Fives. If you are unfamiliar with type Fives, or are struggling to think of their best qualities, here's a little rundown.

Fives are generally observant, focused, objective, and very laid back. As lifelong students, they are often a great source of wisdom on their favorite topics. If any type is the most likely to be introverted, it's Five. They typically don't have the same amount of energy as the rest of us and once their energy is gone, that's it—Fives need to recharge.

A healthy Five not only understands and observes the world, but also enriches others with their knowledge. A healthy Five might still feel the inner panic of the world pulling on their resources, but no longer gives in to its demands as much as they normally would. Branching out socially and making friendships only helps these Fives continue to narrow their expectations for time alone and expand their desire for company. These Fives will be masters in whatever topics pique their interests; they often write books and teach.

It's important to get to know both your stress and growth numbers, One and Five, as a whole. There's no list of qualities or attributes that will fully encompass what you could be gaining from these numbers, but as you learn more about them, you'll often start to recognize that number in yourself. This will help you more easily identify these seasons in your own life.

For most Sevens, going to Five in growth typically looks like:

+ Being able to focus for long periods of time

+ Having healthy curiosity about new topics of interest

+ Being able to slow down and make objective decisions

+ Reaching contentment faster or longing for it in a more productive way

---

SHIFT IN FOCUS

Which quality of Five do you feel like you need most in your life?

Do you feel like a lifelong student?

Who are you the student of?

• • • • • • • • • • • • DAY 53

How Five-ness Enhances Your Seven-ness

*The soul of the sluggard craves and gets nothing,
while the soul of the diligent is richly supplied.*
(Proverbs 13:4)

It's often assumed that laid-back Fives and enthusiastic Sevens are like oil and water—not able to mix very well—but I have found this couldn't be further from the truth.

Fives find Sevens fascinating; they often appreciate their sense of humor and they're frankly glad to have someone else head up conversations. Sevens are often attracted to Fives' knowledge, steadfastness, and contentedness with life at a slower pace. Fives and Sevens are both pretty independent types and they're not offended when the other doesn't need them in order to enjoy themselves.

One of the reasons Fives and Sevens tend to get along is because Sevens have a lot to learn from Fives. It's not that Sevens need to sacrifice their fun nature on the altar of knowledge, or that being a Five is better than being a Seven. Believe me, Fives have their own issues.

However, Five-ness enhances your Seven-ness. If your fun, joyful, bright-sided self harnesses a Five's focus, objectivity, still-ness, and contentment, it's like lighting fireworks.

When Sevens are focused, they not only dream but also make their dreams a reality.

When Sevens are objective, they can make decisions without fear of missing out on something or letting emotions become a deciding factor.

When Sevens are still, they start to feel grateful for what's right in front of them.

And when Sevens are grateful for what's in front of them, they start to encounter God in a marvelous new way.

You are a wonderful, needed reflection of God in your own unique way. But God also made Five-ness the key to your effectiveness in many areas of life.

Adding Five's strengths to your already unstoppable personality will help you become a greater force for good in this world.

SHIFT IN FOCUS

What is it that you admire or respect about the type Fives in your life?

Reread Proverbs 13:4. What does diligence mean to you? Is diligence something you pray for?

• • • • • • • • • • • **DAY 54**

Growing in Focus

> *Commit your work to the* LORD,
> *and your plans will be established.*
> (Proverbs 16:3)

In a nutshell, focus means bringing all of your attention and activity to one point. Sevens are commonly described as being easily distracted and impulsive as they struggle to fix their attention and energy on just one thing. However, dear Seven, when you go to Five in growth, you gain the ability to focus!

You have probably already recognized in your life that if you go into *focus mode*, you can't be stopped, you're more productive than most people are in the same amount of time, and you feel really good about yourself. This is you going to Five.

You probably know more about your topic of interest or extracurricular activities than most people. This is you going to Five.

In order to focus, you cannot be distracted, which can be hard if you live in a busy household or you're quick to respond to the buzzing of your cell phone. However, if you want to grow in focus, you should try to create a distraction-free zone to train yourself to grow in this trait.

How do you do this? Here are some ideas:

- Light a candle and let its scent signal your brain that it's focus time

+ Put on headphones and listen to white noise, soothing sounds, or a specific playlist for focusing so that you're not distracted by trying to select music options

+ Limit your beverage choices—especially if you usually try different flavors at the coffee shop—to take that decision-making effort out of the equation

+ Sit in the same place when you're focusing, whether that's your bed, at a desk, or the same general area of places you frequent

All of these things will condition you to focus by freeing up your mind from having to make a lot of decisions. If necessary, set a timer for thirty minutes and take a break from your phone. That's more productive than being tempted by every buzz. Better still, leave your phone in your car or another room while you try to focus.

SHIFT IN FOCUS

What are a couple of things you need to focus on this week?

How might implementing a distraction-free zone or mental cues help you to focus?

• • • • • • • • • • • **DAY 55**

Growing in Objectivity

For the LORD your God is God of gods and Lord of lords,
the great, the mighty, and the awesome God,
who is not partial and takes no bribe.
(Deuteronomy 10:17)

When we talk about how Enneagram Fives are objective, we mean they're not influenced by personal feelings, interpretations, or prejudice. They can make decisions based on facts and remain unbiased. Obviously, this is not true 100 percent of the time, or for all Fives, but in general, objectivity is considered one of their strengths.

Being objective is a good thing when you need to make big decisions and bias or emotions are high. This is why people often recruit someone who is not biased or emotionally involved in their situation to give them advice. They know they can trust this objective party to look at the facts and suggest a course of action.

For example, you may be offered a new job very far away from where you currently live. The adventure of moving, the pay raise, and the new title are alluring, but it would mean moving away from your parents, your children's schools, and everything you've ever known.

Being objective would help you to weigh the pros and cons of this situation for the good of your family, and listen to what God might be telling you instead of what your loud emotions are shouting.

In the end, either staying or moving could be the right choice, but examining your options objectively can be key to making a decision you won't later regret and give you peace in making it.

Dear Seven, you can start to grow in and practice objectivity by making yourself available to serve as an objective, neutral sounding board for others. Perhaps people have already noticed this strength in you and seek you out for a fresh perspective.

It's also helpful to step back from your own situation when you need to make a decision. Maybe you need to go on a walk or run, go to bed, or even take the weekend off from thinking about it and return to it later. Remind yourself that distance from the initial swell of emotions can help you to think clearer.

Do you need to collect more information before you decide? Other than emotions, what else is impacting your decisions? Are there good schools in the new city? How likely is this promotion to come up again? Listing the advantages and disadvantages can put your decision into perspective and help you make the right choice.

SHIFT IN FOCUS

Do you find that being objective comes easily or hard for you?

In what type of situation does it tend to be harder?

Being unbiased and impartial, especially when giving advice, might seem to be impossible at times, but sometimes, blinds you to the truth. As we see in verses like Deuteronomy 10:17, God is the best impartial judge we have, so go to Him in prayer and seek His counsel.

• • • • • • • • • • **DAY 56**

Growing in Contentment
By Molly Wilcox

Keep your life free from love of money, and be content with what you have, for he has said, "I will never leave you nor forsake you."
(Hebrews 13:5)

One of the most difficult seasons of my life was when my husband and I had just moved across the country. We brought no furniture with us and I soon found myself in an empty apartment in an unfamiliar city, without any family, friends or community, looking to God and wondering where His promise was for us.

I quickly shifted from the excitement of the change and the anticipation of the move of God in our lives to frustration. We felt God call us to move, we felt we were obedient and faithful in picking up our lives for Him, and now where was He? I felt abandoned and hurt.

In this season, God went after my heart in a way He never had before. He took hold of me and taught me in ways I never anticipated. Suddenly, the Holy Spirit guided me through a deeper understanding of who He is. But first, He wanted me to shed some thinking and behaviors that weren't quite right. I became hyper-aware of how entitled I had become.

Before this happened, I was quick to sit around and tell God how deserving I was. I wanted to point out all the ways I was sacrificing for Him and all the things I had given up in my life. I wanted Him to reward me.

Through a long season of quiet reflection with the Lord, I started to shed this spiritual entitlement that I had made a part of my life and shift to true contentment. It wasn't something I did on my own; it was the Holy Spirit working in me, showing me how much He had already given, and allowing me to be content even in my empty apartment, even when I felt His promise was unseen.

I grew in gratitude and ended up feeling so broken for trying to show God how deserving I was. Why was I so focused on asking God for more things? He had already given me so much. He had already sent His Son to die on the cross for me so I could have eternal life. That is truly something that should fill our hearts with gratitude. True contentment is found when we focus on the Father's generous heart for us and see how much He has already provided.

SHIFT IN FOCUS

What are you tempted to think you deserve?

Where in your life do you feel like God is withholding from you? Respond by making a list of ten tangible things for which you are grateful.

Now make a list of ten intangible things for which you are grateful.

Read both lists aloud and thank the Father for His generosity to you.

• • • • • • • • • • • DAY 57

Growing in Self-Reflection
By Molly Wilcox

> *But when you pray, go into your room and shut the door*
> *and pray to your Father who is in secret.*
> *And your Father who sees in secret will reward you.*
> (Matthew 6:6)

Dear Seven, a moment of quiet reflection with your heavenly Father is never wasted. I know it's easier to busy ourselves with coffee dates, small groups, new hobbies, and exciting trips, but I want to challenge you to be brave and sit quietly, alone, with God. During this quiet time alone with Him, you can give yourself space to sift through the thoughts that have been spinning in your mind throughout the day and learn how to slow them down, maybe even quiet them, and listen to Him.

Personally, it's difficult for me to remember to make time for myself. I will easily say yes to going out to lunch and fill my schedule with phone calls with friends, continuously pushing aside *me time*. As much as I love to be in the community, I think it's sometimes a strategy I use to get away from my thoughts. The only way to truly combat this is to make time for self-reflection.

One of the ways I reflect on how I'm feeling, doing, struggling, and growing is through journaling. I journal every day with my morning coffee; here, I am able to admit to myself how I feel and give those feelings over to God. Sometimes, I confess, I think it's wrong to feel negative emotions. In my quiet times of reflection, I am able to tell myself the truth that God is willing and able to handle *all* of my emotions, on any side of the spectrum. When I take time to journal and pray, I become more self-aware in a profound way. I am able to see who I am as a child of God. This time of reflection always results in growth.

The challenge for me isn't knowing that it's good for me to take time to reflect, but actually doing it. I almost always feel like there's a better offer on the table, and I'd rather say yes to a latte at my local coffee shop with a friend than time on my own. But once I make time, I grow, so I can see its value.

We Sevens become better at self-reflection as we go to Five in growth. These times become more productive as we grow in focus, discipline, and objectivity. Let's challenge each other to be brave enough to make the time to be alone with God and our thoughts.

SHIFT IN FOCUS

Is self-reflection or time alone with God something you do on a daily or weekly basis? Why or why not?

Commit to time alone this week. Schedule it as you would do for a fun, exciting activity and then tell someone who can hold you accountable to following through. Don't be afraid to commit! Use the time to spend in self-reflection in a way that works for you. Try journaling or listening to soothing instrumental music.

• • • • • • • • • • • • **DAY 58**

Growing Through Quiet
By Molly Wilcox

Be still, and know that I am God.
I will be exalted among the nations, I will be exalted in the earth!
(Psalm 46:10)

When I was in college, I had an opportunity to attend a silent weekend retreat. I don't think I really knew what I was signing up for, but all of my friends were going and I didn't want to miss out.

After we arrived at the retreat center where we were staying, I realized that we were literally going to be practicing silence as a spiritual discipline for *days*. It sounded terrifying to me.

In the beginning, I felt like I was a part of an experiment. Could a bunch of college kids actually be quiet? Then, it started to feel like a waste of time. There were rules—no technology, for instance—but somehow, I was able to persevere.

I remember finding a quiet chapel. Much to my surprise, it was empty, so I sat in the still, silent protection of its walls on a rainy Saturday, watching the rain through the stained glass windows. I sat there alone for hours. Time went by and I somehow made it through that silent retreat, even eating meals without speaking to anyone.

In the silence, God restored my soul. I felt closer to Him than ever before, safe and confident in His presence in a new way. I had no idea silence could have such a profound impact on me. Later, I told my friends that I wanted to implement times of silence in my life on a regular basis. The retreat was an unexpected blessing.

Silence is something that is so opposite of who I am—and I'm guessing that as a fellow Seven, it's rare for you too. I have a lot to say all the time and no one's ever asked me, "Why are you so quiet?" I am always ready to bring the party, filled with energy, and brimming with stories and laughter.

Silence challenges me to put away the external voices, even my own, and rest in who God is. It strips the world bare of distractions and causes me to hear what all of the noise may be accidentally drowning out. It forces me to listen to the soft, gentle truths, turning my focus to the world with a renewed sense of vision, to see what might have been missed amid distractions.

SHIFT IN FOCUS

Find a space where you can have an intentional time of silence. It might be a quiet room in your home, your car, a nearby park, or even going to your workplace before starting time. Set a timer and be quiet. Don't use technology or listen to music or a podcast. Eliminate distractions and practice silence as a spiritual discipline. Begin with a length of time that feels like a stretch, but isn't too big of a challenge. Be still and focused on God's presence.

• • • • • • • • • • • **DAY 59**

The Focused Seven
By Molly Wilcox

But his delight is in the law of the LORD,
and on his law he meditates day and night.
(Psalm 1:2)

As a Seven, I have often been put into a box labeled "easily distracted, scatterbrained, and quick to move from one thing to the next." Honestly, sometimes that hurts. I am interested in many different things and I have come to realize that this is often a strength. I believe God made us as Sevens to be able to shift our focus quickly from one thing to the next. We love to learn, we are often picking up new hobbies, and we can master something new quickly when it intrigues us.

There is a difference between being interested in multiple things and being too distracted to focus on any one thing. As I have grown, I've come to realize that when my focus is first and foremost on the Father, the rest becomes clear and falls into place. I have a deep fascination with God's Word. While in college, I worked for the Center for Scripture Engagement and I began to research and write about the Bible during that time.

I quickly became engrossed in the Scriptures. I desired to know more, understand more, and truly have God's Word in my heart. I love this verse from the first Psalm because it talks about meditating on the Word day and night. As a Seven, when I become fixated on something, it can take my entire focus, and

I think that's a way God wants us to relate to Him. I think He wants us to look to Him for focus; when we do, the world around us becomes clearer. This type of focus is a strength of Fives and something that can become a strength of us Sevens in seasons of growth.

When we see things as God sees them, He can highlight for us how He made us and how He desires for us to spend our time. It starts with a focus on Him, and then He equips and prepares us to focus fully on giving our gifts and talents back to Him like an offering. When we focus on Him and on His heart for the world around us, it becomes clear how we can use our time wisely and help the world around us. When our focus is on the Father, He can give us vision and focus for the ways He desires to use us in our communities.

SHIFT IN FOCUS

Pick a passage of Scripture that speaks to you and read it a few times slowly so that your mind can rest on that Word. With this message from God in your mind, go for a walk. Don't bring technology or distractions along with you, but simply take a walk while you mull over the passage you have read. Allow God to use this focused time with you and enjoy being in the world with Him.

• • • • • • • • • • • • DAY 60

The Growing Seven

Practice these things, immerse yourself in them,
so that all may see your progress.
(1 Timothy 4:15)

At first, prioritizing growth may feel like jumping off a cliff. Every moment you are convicted to act and don't, the reality of acting becomes scarier in your head. Again and again, you may fail to take the leap because it just feels too hard, and then you'll feel beaten down and *not enough*.

Dear Seven, this is the challenge of being motivated by satisfaction. You might always wonder if the discipline, stillness, and focus aspects of Fives are making you miss out on what will truly satisfy you. This feeling is something Satan uses to make sure you never walk in the freedom of your worth in Christ.

Our adversary is all about stopping your growth from coming to fruition. I wouldn't be surprised if you even notice elements of spiritual attack as you prioritize growth. *But that doesn't mean the growth isn't God's heart for you.*

Choosing growth instead of the next fun thing may feel painful at times and you may get discouraged. Please remember that life is seasonal and you will not achieve your *ultimate* state of growth here on earth. You cannot become your ideal self because you will never be without a sin nature while you're still drawing a breath. However, you *are* growing; by the power of the Holy

Spirit, you are in the process of becoming the person God created you to be.

Don't let two steps forward and one step back discourage you. This is still moving forward. This is still growth.

When you choose to rest, you're trusting God that you will be satisfied. You're trusting that focusing might be better than the temptation of distraction. You're agreeing with the psalmist who wrote, *"God is the strength of my heart and my portion forever"* (Psalm 73:26). You're trusting that your feelings might not always be telling you the truth. And like a child at the edge of the swimming pool jumping into their father's arms, you're trusting that God is ready to catch you.

SHIFT IN FOCUS

> *Practice these things, immerse yourself in them, so that all may see your progress.*   (1 Timothy 4:15)

We are going to use this verse as a guideline for action.

"Practice these things"

Every new thing you've ever done required practice. Growing by going to Five is no different. Practice and have a plan for focus, plan for stillness or purposeful alone time, and choose one action that can be your next right thing. Every small step counts.

"Immerse yourself in them"

What verse that we mentioned over the last ten days really stuck out to you? I would encourage you to memorize it, write it out, and place it somewhere so that you will see it every day. Immerse yourself in the truth of your worth in Christ, and you'll find yourself slowly but surely believing it to be true.

"So that all may see your progress"

Pick a couple people in your life to share your big or small victories with. I hope you have a few come to mind right away, but if they don't, there are plenty of Instagram or Facebook pages for Sevens who would love to cheer you on in your Seven-ish wins. Be bold and share them as something worth celebrating. After a few hours of focus, go out for a coffee, or have a bowl of ice cream! Life is hard, and any victories are worth celebrating with God and others.

BOOK RECOMMENDATIONS FOR SEVENS

Larry Crabb, *A Different Kind of Happiness: Discovering the Joy That Comes from Sacrificial Love* (Grand Rapids, MI: Baker Books, 2016)

Linda Dillow, *Satisfy My Thirsty Soul: For I Am Desperate for Your Presence* (Colorado Springs, CO: NavPress, 2007)

Kate Merrick, *And Still She Laughs: Defiant Joy in the Depths of Suffering* (Nashville, TN: Nelson Books, 2017)

Michelle Van Loon, *Born to Wander: Recovering the Value of Our Pilgrim Identity* (Chicago, IL: Moody Publishers, 2018)

Tish Harrison Warren, *Liturgy of the Ordinary: Sacred Practices in Everyday Life* (Downers Grove, IL: InterVarsity Press, 2016)

Shauna Niequist, *Present Over Perfect: Leaving Behind Frantic for a Simpler, More Soulful Way of Living* (Grand Rapids, MI: Zondervan, 2016)

Aundi Kolber, *Try Softer: A Fresh Approach to Move Us out of Anxiety, Stress, and Survival Mode—and into a Life of Connection and Joy* (Carol Stream, IL: Tyndale House Publishers, 2020)

Jen Wilkin, *None Like Him: 10 Ways God Is Different from Us (and Why That's a Good Thing)* (Wheaton, IL: Crossway, 2016)

Ingrid Fetell Lee, *Joyful: The Surprising Power of Ordinary Things to Create Extraordinary Happiness* (New York, NY: Little, Brown Spark, 2018)

―――――――――――――

As the Enneagram has passed through many hands, and been taught by various wonderful people, I want to acknowledge that none of the concepts or ideas of the Enneagram have been created by me. I'd like to give thanks to the Enneagram teachers and pioneers who have gone before me, and whose work has influenced this devotional:

Suzanne Stabile

Ian Morgan Cron

Father Richard Rhor

Don Richard Riso

Russ Hudson

Beatrice Chestnut

Beth McCord

Ginger Lapid-Bogda

ABOUT THE AUTHOR

Elisabeth Bennett first discovered the Enneagram in the summer of 2017 and immediately realized how life-changing this tool could be. She set out to absorb all she could about this ancient personality typology, including a twelve-week Enneagram Certification course taught by Beth McCord, who has studied the Enneagram for more than twenty-five years.

Elisabeth started her own Enneagram Instagram account (@Enneagram.Life) in 2018, which has grown to nearly 65,000 followers. Since becoming a certified Enneagram coach, Elisabeth has conducted more than one hundred one-on-one coaching sessions to help her clients find their type and apply the Enneagram to their lives for personal and spiritual growth. She has also conducted staff/team building sessions for businesses and high school students.

Elisabeth has lived in beautiful Washington State her entire life and now has the joy of raising her own children there with her husband, Peter.

To contact Elisabeth, please visit:

www.elisabethbennettenneagram.com

www.instagram.com/enneagram.life